The best memoirs tell a story that is
and yet somehow transcends partic⎡
story of one man's pain and growth
his son's diagnosis with autism, and at the same time, this
book invites me into reflection about my own experience
with pain, denial, hope, and healing. As this father begins
to let go of fear and open his heart up to trust, I, too, am
invited to explore all the ways I have shut myself off from
the ache, and the joy, of full life.

AMY JULIA BECKER, author of *White Picket Fences* and *A Good and Perfect Gift*

Honest, wise, beautiful. After I lost a dear friend, *Aching Joy*
was precisely what I needed to read. Jason Hague's honesty
about his own failings, doubts, and questions about God
in a painful season of his family's life made me feel like I
wasn't alone. His insights, wisdom, and sensitivity to God
gave me hope. I cried multiple times reading this book.
Highly recommended.

MATT MIKALATOS, author of *Good News for a Change* and *Sky Lantern*

Sometimes we beg God for an answer to prayer and don't
receive it. Then what? Hague writes with raw honesty about
his son's autism diagnosis—and the prayer requests denied.
I don't know the source of your begging (mine was different
from Hague's), but you'll grow through the universal wisdom
found in this book, which helps readers see that God is still
in the story—and that our circumstances don't get to decide
our levels of joy. A new kind of joy—an aching joy—awaits.

SEPTEMBER VAUDREY, author of *Colors of Goodbye*

Jason accomplishes the extraordinary: He teaches and shares wisdom without condescension. He preaches without being preachy. With honesty and humility, he shares the unvarnished, unfiltered challenges that confront every special-needs parent and the wisdom that is earned through facing those challenges with honest personal and spiritual reflection. His love for his family drips from every page, and the wisdom he shares translates to anyone facing a critical life challenge. This is an important book and an important message. I'm honored to call him my friend.

JERRY TURNING, JR. (MR. BACON), blogger at *Bacon and Juice Boxes: Our Life with Autism*

Jason Hogue is a modern-day psalmist. His words ring with courage, honesty, transparency, and raw beauty. He shines a light in the darkness to remind us that every single emotion is safe before a sovereign God who is big enough to hold all the pieces.

TRICIA LOTT WILLIFORD, author of *And Life Comes Back* and *You Can Do This*

When followers of Jesus face devastating pain, unanswered prayer, and dashed hopes, Jason Hague says Western Christianity offers two options: a pious, naive, praise-the-Lord-anyway optimism or a realistic, resigned, *Where are you, God?* despair. Through the raw story of his relationship with his son Jack, who wrestles with autism, Hague offers another path: courageously walking alongside a relentlessly loving Father into a life of deep mystery—the mystery of fully embracing both the hopeful, redemptive dreams of victory and the disappointment of unexplained, bleeding-out defeat. In other words, a mysterious, powerful life of . . . aching joy.

J. KEVIN BUTCHER, author of *Choose and Choose Again*

My family's story and Jason's family's story are very similar, but the themes of *Aching Joy* are universal. We all wonder what God is up to in times of hardship, especially when it seems to go on for years. Jason's transparency is a gift that shows us how to live with both joy and longing. His courage to share his experiences gives me courage to keep holding on to God as I raise my son, who has Level 3 autism. Following Jason's example, I can rejoice in my hopes, be patient in my trials, and persevere in my prayers, as the apostle Paul instructs us.

SANDRA PEOPLES, MDiv, author of *Unexpected Blessings*

Jason Hague's book, *Aching Joy*, is for anyone whose dreams have at one time turned to rubble in "the Land of Unanswered Prayer," which is "just east of Acceptance and west of Breakthrough." It is *also* for parents of children who have special needs (or their friends), or anyone who walks alongside families with a loved one on the autism spectrum. The struggles Hague's son experiences trying to express his inner world, as well as the turmoil Hague describes in his efforts to truly have a relationship with his son, ring with gritty honesty and give no easy answers. But there is beauty and redemption. As Hague moves through the graveyard of his hopes, while still believing—or trying to believe—in an almighty Father who can move mountains, he gains insights into "incarnational parenting" that are full of startling joy—and hope—for us all, whatever our journeys.

ELIZABETH BERG, MA, special education, and principal of James Irwin Charter Elementary School

ACHING JOY

ACHING JOY

FOLLOWING GOD THROUGH THE
LAND OF UNANSWERED PRAYER

NAVPRESS®

*A NavPress resource published in alliance
with Tyndale House Publishers, Inc.*

NavPress is the publishing ministry of The Navigators, an international Christian organization and leader in personal spiritual development. NavPress is committed to helping people grow spiritually and enjoy lives of meaning and hope through personal and group resources that are biblically rooted, culturally relevant, and highly practical.

For more information, visit www.NavPress.com.

The Team: Don Pape, Publisher; Caitlyn Carlson, Acquisitions Editor; Elizabeth Symm, Copy Editor; Daniel Farrell, Designer

Cover illustration of people silhouette copyright © dovla982/Shutterstock; all rights reserved. Cover illustration of sunset by Daniel Farrell, copyright © Tyndale House Publishers, Inc.; all rights reserved. Author photo by Anne Nunn Photographers, copyright © 2018; all rights reserved.

Published in association with William K. Jensen Literary Agency, 119 Bampton Ct., Eugene, OR 97404

For Emily, Jenna, Sam, and Nathan:

Jack's Honor Guard and my Psalms of Hope

Contents

Though giant rains put out the sun,

    Here stand I for a sign.

Though Earth be filled with waters dark,

    My cup is filled with wine.

Tell to the trembling priests that here

    Under the deluge rod,

One nameless, tattered, broken man

    Stood up and drank to God.

G. K. CHESTERTON, "THE DELUGE"

Introduction

The Night I Hit the Ground

THERE'S A CLASSIC GAG in old cartoons where a character steps off a desert cliff but keeps on walking. He can go on like that forever as long as he doesn't realize he's treading on air. The audience is in on the joke, of course, long before the character is. Everyone knows that as soon as the poor soul looks down, it's all over. He will try to turn around. He will flail and claw and swim the empty space in an effort to grab the ledge, but gravity will snag his toe just before he succeeds. And then, with great fanfare, comes the crash.

I feel an unsettling familiarity when I watch this scene play out. I can relate to this character. This fall. It has happened to me. Indeed, it has happened to many of us, especially to those of us who are Christians, who think we know where our hearts ought to be in times of crisis and imagine ourselves there. We need the solid ground of settledness and security, so we invent it. We need emotional stability and firm faith, so we smile and tell ourselves God will handle it. Those who know us and love us best can see it coming a mile away: We're about to crash.

My crash came one February night at a church conference. It was late—almost ten o'clock. The speaker was a bald, well-mannered Englishman whom I normally enjoyed, but not at this hour. Not when we still had to drive ninety minutes to get home.

When he called the worship band back onstage, I perked up. Maybe he was about to land the plane. But no, he wasn't sitting down. He was pacing. Something else was on his mind; something he hadn't been teaching on.

"If you are the parent of a special-needs child, I'd like you to come up and get prayer."

I grunted. Not that. Come on; that's not fair.

I scanned the area for an escape route, and I found one. I could take it without making the slightest disruption. The only obstacle between me and that back door was the team of church staff who had come with me to the conference.

But I didn't need prayer. I was fine. I mean, not fine fine, but at least I wasn't depressed like I had been. Years earlier, when my son Jack's regressive autism first set in, he had gone into a fog, and I had gone into one too. I had walked the common path of grief, starting with denial and lingering for years in depression. During that long season, I needed tons of prayer. But now I was okay; I had reached "acceptance." My personal malaise was over. My feet were on solid ground.

And yet our church staff were sitting behind me, the

ones who had held up my arms during those darker times. They would see me, and they would give me the collective stink eye if I walked out; it would have been their right. I owed them this.

A long line of young ministry students formed at the front of the stage, eager to pounce on any pitiful parent who dared come forward. This was a zealous bunch too. They would pray loud, sweaty prayers. I dragged myself forward, choosing a tall Canadian man in a brown, businesslike sweater. I had heard him talk earlier, and he seemed safe enough—the kind who might not yell too much when talking with the Almighty.

"My son Jack has severe autism," I told him beneath the cover of ringing synthesizers. "He's seven, and he can't speak and . . . yeah . . ." I stopped there to brace myself for an explosion of fervent perspiration, but it never came. Instead, my Canadian closed his eyes and started to whisper. I had to lean in to hear. He sounded gentle and confident, a prince next to his Father's throne.

And then it happened. He said the word *breakthrough*, and I crumbled into myself, weeping.

Breakthrough. That word—it was all I had asked for. Such a small request, it seemed, from the God who could hold galaxies in his fingertips and make seas stand with his breath. I hadn't prayed for anything as big as that . . . just a little breakthrough. There was a wall between me and my son, and I wanted a hole punched through it.

For years, my wife and I had begged God to "fix" our

son's autism, and at first, we thought he would do it. We had both grown up in God-soaked environments. I was a minister's son in the Bible Belt, surrounded by missionaries who had seen miracles firsthand. Sara was a preacher's daughter in rural Minnesota, full of the faith and confidence that can only come from one who has eavesdropped on counseling sessions that morphed into exorcisms in her own living room. God had healed my mom from severe back problems and had healed Sara's mom from polio. Faith was in our blood.

We carried those stories into adulthood, more or less convinced that God was capable of anything. But thus far, he hadn't answered our most desperate prayer: Jack was still nonverbal. He had grown some, learning a few new skills here and there, but the developmental gap between him and his peers was widening, not shrinking. At age three, the diagnosis had read "moderate autism." At seven, it read "severe." The truth was settling in on me: Our prayers weren't working. Jack's condition was getting worse.

I wanted to get mad at God, but I didn't have the theological conviction to make it stick. Frankly, I wasn't sure what God's role was in Jack's condition. Certainly, I believed that all things—even hard things—"work together for good to those who love God" (Romans 8:28). But did that mean he caused all the hard things in the first place? I didn't think so. In my mind, that was just how redemption worked: God made beauty from ashes, but the ashes themselves didn't necessarily flow from his hand.

Thus, it seemed to me I had two choices: I could either live in perpetual sadness or lower my level of hope. For ages I had embraced the first option, but it was costly. My personality had changed during my walk through depression, the fourth stage of grief. I had become distant and numb, and my family was suffering because of it. I had to pull out of that for the sake of us all. The only option left, then, was for me to lower my expectations and embrace my new normal in hopes that God might salvage something out of it. It was a weak embrace of Romans 8:28, but an embrace nonetheless.

From there, I resigned myself to minimizing disappointment. I started asking God for an easier, more realistic breakthrough. Jack would never converse, I decided, but he might at least learn to bathe himself with soap and shampoo.

And little by little, the new posture worked. Soon I found I had come to terms with Jack's condition. We were playing together and laughing together like never before. Even on bad days, when he might be in the middle of an epic meltdown, I could still feel peace. Joy, even. By lowering my expectations, I had found solid ground. My life was beginning to make sense again.

But all that ended the night my Canadian whispered "breakthrough." He exposed me with his prayer. I was grief stained and empty—again. It was a humiliating self-revelation. Had anything ever changed inside me? Had I ever really let go of any expectations? Despite my best efforts, I was still a snotty mess craving "breakthrough" more than anything else in the world—and still not getting it.

But how could I help it? How could I be satisfied when my son was still distant from me? I missed him. Why hadn't he emerged from that dim place? Where were the sunbursts of language? Where was that relationship he was made for? And, dear God, what would happen to him in the tomorrows?

చ

My story is not your story, but we all share this kind of disorienting pain to some degree. The uncertainty of our everyday lives ought to be a given, but in the Western evangelical church, it is more like a shameful secret. We hunger for resolution and thirst for certainty. We crave the security that comes from airtight theological postulates. We sing the grateful anthems of the psalmists, all the while ignoring the laments they wrote before God rescued them. I fear we move through this hymnal too quickly, relating only to the victories and not the struggles. They were as real as ours.

And so I wonder whether it is harder sometimes for Christians like me to deal with the inevitable flooding. We grew up in Sunday school, see, so we know we are supposed to be "inside, outside, upside, downside happy all the time." We've "got the joy, joy, joy, joy" down in our hearts. "Where?"

Somewhere down there. It's there somewhere.

"You boys look so cute in your Sunday clothes! How

are you doing this morning?" the big-haired ladies would ask my brothers and me. And there was only one correct answer: "We're doing fine."

Fine. That's what we call the ground where we think we ought to be standing—the ground of Fine. We imagine ourselves there, and we keep walking: Eyes up. Smile on. Don't look down. Don't admit your open wounds, your hanging doubts, your naked needs.

I am a pastor. I'm not supposed to have naked needs. I'm not supposed to look down. But I looked down and realized I had unfinished business with God. The reality of my condition rushed up at me like the hot desert sands. That fall broke me, and it continues to break me.

Today, I am still living in the country I fell into: the Land of Unanswered Prayer. It lies just east of Acceptance and west of Breakthrough. Maybe you're here, too, living with lingering pains and troubles that refuse to resolve. Maybe there's an illness. A death. A severed relationship. Whatever it is, it's not going away, and you want to know why God hasn't made it better. Your heart throbs—maybe with anger, maybe with hurt—but almost certainly with disappointment.

We now have to choose: We can either climb back up to the invisible path of forced smiles or stay on this parched earth and wallow in our broken states. We only have those two choices.

Or do we?

Of all the false binaries in our modern, angry world,

this one might be the most damaging. Why must we decide between happiness and sorrow, denial and despair, the joy and the aching? It is a wrong idea that exaggerates both the bright side and the dark: the bright side, full of sunshine, and the dark side, grim as death. The premise requires that we pledge allegiance between two extreme views of the world, two straw men that can offer nothing more than safe, intellectual predictability.

For some of us, this predictability is precisely what makes these options attractive. There is something safe in the formula of a tragic romance. To know life is hard and then we die—at least we can count on that. Or conversely, to convince ourselves there's nothing to be sad about, and everything is as it ought to be . . . that's a relief as well. Fatalism helps us all to sigh more deeply.

But the sighs of safety and predictability are such small prizes. What if there was a third way forward that offered more than mere predictability?

The way is out there. And it does, indeed, offer much more. In fact, there are treasures waiting to be found. God promised this through his prophet Isaiah: "I will give you treasures hidden in the darkness—secret riches. I will do this so you may know that I am the Lord, the God of Israel, the one who calls you by name" (Isaiah 45:3, NLT).

This is a book about the treasures I found in my darkness, and the greatest of all was this: aching joy. The Lord taught me how to sigh in pain, how to weep in gladness, and how to trust during days of hope deferred. It was not an easy road to walk. It still isn't easy, and it isn't safe. Rather, it is a confounding country full of myths and mirages. Here, faith resembles denial, settledness looks like surrender, and hope is the scariest creature of all.

But this book is also about you. If you are with me here in the Land of Unanswered Prayer, you know all about discouragement. But look up, friend. The path before us is paved with secret riches. To embrace it is to embrace the terrifying tension of God's inaugurated but unfinished Kingdom: the already and the not yet, the treasure in the field costing us everything but giving us even more. It is the place where I thank God for my son, who is enough, and in the next breath, I beg God for more.

The road ahead is dangerous but not barren. There is sustenance here, because Christ himself is here, and he goes before us. He walked this path already, this Man of Sorrows, and endured all that we must endure and more. But he did it all "for the joy set before Him" (Hebrews 12:2, NASB).

On this journey, we will follow his lead. He does not hover above us on the winds of false expectations. Rather, he stands next to us with his own humble scars, beckoning us forward.

If we come this way, our expectations may need recalibration. Our long-held daydreams may need to be released. Life won't look the way we thought it would, but he has prepared a path for us, complete with breath-stopping vistas; cool, crystal streams; and pleasures for the soul.

This is my story. This is our story. Come, journey with me.

PART I

Embracing the Aching

ᕧ

CHAPTER 1

Our Precious Propaganda

IT ALL STARTED WITH DAYDREAMS. Maybe that was my problem. My glowing expectations of fatherhood created the perfect setup for my original disappointment with God.

Jack tried to escape his mother's womb on Super Bowl Sunday, 2006, and he almost succeeded. Sara's water broke in the second quarter of the Steelers versus Seahawks matchup, but she told me I could watch the rest of the game before we left for the delivery. Because our two daughters, Emily and Jenna, had both taken their own sweet time on their birthdays, she figured our new son would take at least a few more hours to get serious about coming out. Still, her offer seemed like a trap. If I accepted it, the story would surely be told for years to come, and I doubted any woman would ever let me live it down.

We met the midwife at something called a "birthing center," an old house that wanted very much to remind clients they were not in the hospital. Candles were already flickering their soft light, and Thomas Kinkade paintings were standing watch over the floral wallpaper. Sara settled down for a while on a hefty blue medicine ball while I massaged her back and tried not to think of the game. The Steelers were probably running away with it anyway.

After thirty minutes of bobbing and deep breathing, we moved into the expanded bathroom, where my wife soaked in a steaming tub smelling of lavender. The bath salts were supposed to help her body relax, but it was a hopeless endeavor from the start. How could she possibly relax? There was a prisoner inside her trying to dig his way out like Andy Dufresne in *The Shawshank Redemption*.

The midwife left us alone for a while. We didn't say much—I just rubbed Sara's shoulders and smiled. Soon it would all be over. Tomorrow our new child would be here: my first son. Finally. He and I could christen our relationship by watching the Super Bowl on VHS, and it would be so suspenseful!

"The Steelers won the game," the midwife said, reemerging without warning. I grunted.

But there was no time for sulking. The fullness of time had come, and I moved my tired wife, who was greater than ever with child, to a regular guest room with a regular bed and lots of quilts that wouldn't be seen in a sterile hospital. There, she began to push.

We whispered our encouragements, the midwife and I, because anything above a whisper would drown out Sara's quiet moaning. I figured she had earned every one of those moans. I had seen this process twice already, and while it is undoubtedly sacred, it is anything but beautiful. No, childbirth is sheer pain and messy fire. And for the third time, Sara was doing it all without meds. It hurt just watching her. I thought I might need her epidural.

The boy gave us some drama near the end, spending so much time in the birth canal that we nearly called for the ambulance. But then in an instant, he was sucking air and sobbing like a champ, covered in that familiar wet clay all newborns wear. Our voices finally rose enough to celebrate at their regular volume—but not too much louder, for it was after midnight.

Nine pounds, seven ounces. We named him "Jackson" after my grandfather, and "Landry" after the legendary Dallas Cowboys coach. We would call him Jack, mostly because of Jack Bauer, the famed anti-terrorism agent on our favorite TV show, *24*.

My son's name and the time of his appearance both seemed preordained: He and I would be the all-American duo, playing catch in the backyard and shooting hoops after dark. There would be Star Wars viewings, paintball showdowns, and Narnia read-alouds. We would grow together, arguing theology over hot coffee and eating Whataburger while watching *Seinfeld* reruns. Just me and my boy.

In hindsight, it is easy to label these visions as inherently selfish, and they might have been. They were mostly about me, after all. But then, throughout history, dads have always reveled in their sons' future exploits. Men don't want children for the general continuation of the human species. That's way too broad for most of us. No, we want to reproduce a certain kind of life. Our kind. Our family culture.

Of course, the fact that these desires are universal does not mean they are virtuous or even helpful, but they are at least inborn. I never had to conjure up my little movies. The reels were already in my head, waiting to project my expectations in dazzling high definition.

I have a theory about such expectations. If we would just get in the habit of acknowledging them, I think we'd be okay when hard times hit. If we could transfer our mental films to the real world—if we could write them down or speak them aloud—we might at least see them for what they are: subjective, childish daydreams. Then we could blush a little. After all, do we really think life is going to be pain free? Of course not. It never is.

But that's not what most of us do. Most of us embrace these visions in hushed solitude. We huddle in the glow of our invented fantasies and pray the projector stays on. Our expectations indoctrinate our minds like propaganda films, seeping into our subconscious with their laughable utopian ideals. Then, when life's emergency alarms start blaring, we panic like those who have never gone through the fire drill.

Maybe you were like me, or maybe you had a better grip on reality. Whatever the case, as we begin this journey through the Land of Unanswered Prayer, we need to interrogate the expectations we started with. These are the perceived injustices that pushed us to pray with such desperation in the first place. Were we being realistic? Did we somehow think we would be exempt from hard times because of our standing with Christ?

My daydreams were probably brighter than most people's because I had it easy growing up. Mom and Dad told me daily that they loved me and weekly that they were proud of me. My teachers were personal cheerleaders, and my friends crossed oceans with me to tell people about Jesus. Indeed, my world was a positive Christian cocoon where people said things like "God loves you and wants to take you on an adventure." And I never doubted either part of that statement, because my soul had never been stepped on.

The fact is, I knew nothing of crisis. My friends had experienced all manner of pain, whereas I had somehow managed to dodge it at every turn. Familial rejection, extreme poverty, and death were all foreigners, and I didn't speak their language. By the time I was twenty-one, the only person I'd ever lost was my grandpa, and he was ninety-one years old. That was hardly a tragedy; he was just worn out.

Life was good, and I knew God was good. So naturally, I
followed my parents' example by going into ministry. A few
years after Sara and I were married, we joined a missions
agency. My job was to work with the Bible school program.
I helped train missionaries from around the globe in the
most practical themes of Scripture—the nature of sin, the
nature of salvation, and especially, the character of God:

> The LORD, the LORD God, compassionate
> and gracious, slow to anger, and abounding in
> lovingkindness and truth.
>
> EXODUS 34:6, NASB

We majored on those words, God's self-description to
Moses, and we followed the thread throughout the Old and
New Testaments. I taught this theme with energy and pas-
sion, and to most people, I was pretty convincing.

Some of those faces, though . . . You know the ones—
flat eyes dropping to notebooks, jaws shifting to the left,
blank and unemotional stares—they represented the hold-
outs. They were listening because they wanted to believe,
but none of my fast-talking exegesis could erase the giant
questions engraved on their souls:

If God is really good, then why?

Why did my mom have to die in that accident?

*Why didn't God protect me when my uncle would come
to visit?*

Why can't we have children?

I kept an academic distance from those questions. In my mind, they were puzzles, not pains, and I knew that might be a problem someday. In fact, I was all too aware that crisis might find me eventually, and its teeth would be deadly. Would I be able to withstand the attack? And when it was over, would I still believe in the goodness of God?

Those nagging concerns started way back in high school, and they grew only more intense after I married Sara. She was so lovely and gracious and forgiving that I started to wonder if a shoe was going to drop. Then we produced two blond beauties who acted out fairy tales and could speak Elizabethan English. My girls were smart, charming, and thoroughly healthy.

The promise of health had become so prominent that I never realized how powerful it was. I don't think I'm alone here. I suspect this is the main reason we Westerners are so inept at dealing with pain. It is why our medications turn quickly into addictions. We are accustomed to a healthy, pain-free existence. Wellness has become the standard backdrop to our propagandist daydreams, where our families live cozy little lives and our children are perpetually whole.

Classic marriage vows promise a different fate. Phrases like "for better or for worse" and "in sickness and in health" remind us that our bodies are fragile and a life in comfort is never guaranteed. Maybe it would help to take a similar vow on the day our children are born. Not that it would make us love them any more, but we might at least take seriously the possibilities that life won't give us unlimited games of H.O.R.S.E. in the driveway.

I believe our expectations need recalibrating, especially for those of us who follow Jesus in such wealthy nations. Too many preachers feed our anxious souls with soaring promises of prosperity and wholeness. They maintain that a God who is eternally good would want the best for his children.

Surely this must be true. God defined himself as good in the Old Testament, and in the New, John the Evangelist summed up what he saw as obvious: "God is love" (1 John 4:8). John, of all people, should know. He was, after all, himself "the disciple whom [Jesus] loved" (John 19:26).

But even John, who knew firsthand the generous affections of the Savior, had no illusions about trouble-free lives for saints. He saw Christ naked and penniless and hanging from a Roman tree. John knew the sting of good expectations gone bad, and he felt the hot tears of a grieving mother on his neck.

That wasn't all. Even when all those tears turned to laughter, John lived the rest of his days as a religious minority in a hostile empire. His own people had rejected him, and after years of faithfulness, the Romans dipped his body into scalding hot oil, expecting him to die. When he didn't, a rumor spread that he had obtained immortality. Can you imagine the burns he had to carry with him the rest of his life?

John lived out his final days in exile on the island prison

of Patmos, apart from his former companions. Tradition holds that every other original disciple met a martyr's death. John alone, with his throbbing patches of aged red skin, died of natural causes.[1] If John held to the same manic expectations that plague us in modern America, he gave us no indication of it. Rather, he assured us of a life of trouble. John's Gospel was the only one to quote this sobering assurance from Jesus:

> I have said these things to you, that in me you may have peace. In the world you will have tribulation. But take heart; I have overcome the world.
>
> JOHN 16:33, ESV

There are no illusions in this warning. Our world is filled with tribulation: sickness, poverty, famine, war, and death. This land is still broken in a thousand different ways. Jesus makes it clear that we will taste that brokenness. Period. That is just as true for suburban graphic designers as for AIDS orphans in Kolkata. There is no incantation to ward off trouble, no declaration or secret prayer that will shield us from tears and bloodstains. There is only the assurance that peace resides in Christ, so we must too.

When I first held my sticky newborn son that night, I wish I had understood this. Before I ever heard the word *autism*, I wish I had looked ahead with Jesus-style realism. I wish I had pondered what it means to walk through a broken world behind the one whose body was broken for me. I wish I had switched off the projector now and then, because my daydreams were about to lie to me. To date, I have never shot baskets with my son. He doesn't watch Star Wars with me, and we don't converse about theology or action thrillers. As much as I would like to blame my disappointment on the general brokenness of our world, I can't do it. That wouldn't be fair. Some of my pain was self-inflicted. After all, I was the one who kept playing those movies in my head. It wasn't necessarily a sin, but it was a tactical mistake that stung for years.

If you are grappling with your own broken daydreams, can I encourage you to do something? Turn off the projector. You don't have to burn the footage. I tried that myself, and it backfired. I'll talk about that in a later chapter. But for now, just turn off the film. Stop watching it. It isn't helping you anymore.

Since the early days of my struggle, I have become convinced of this: Our expectations cannot grow in the shifting soils of circumstance. Only in the unchanging, eternal Christ can peace truly flourish. In him, our expectations become secondary to his. Our riches will rust and our health will forsake us, but he has sworn to do no such thing. Ever. In Christ alone, our visions are free to grow wild, for he himself is freedom, and his very name is Love.

CHAPTER 2

A Gathering Storm

NONE OF US CAME to the Land of Unanswered Prayer unbidden. The storms sent us all. The clouds gathered dark and low, and a rumbling began both in our skies and in our bones. Then came the rains, the fog, the floods; the questions and accusations, disorientation, and groaning too deep for words. Once our worlds were all atumble, we arrived here as refugees, carrying memories we salvaged from the deluge.

For instance, I have an old pixelated video of twelve-month-old Jack learning to walk. Like a tipsy teddy bear, he is stumbling back and forth between me and his two sisters, his mouth wide with triumph and his eyes alive with cloudless laughter. Sara is behind the camera, offering whoops of victory, and all four of us are cheering.

There is enough distance between me and that little clip to make me feel like a disinterested spectator at a museum exhibit dedicated to normal families of the twenty-first century. I recognize the little blond girls—their faces are the same—but I hardly know the other two. The thin man with the weak beard seems so alive. So engaged and happy. There are no wrinkles on his face, no shadows clouding his brow. Just grayless optimism and glory. And the boy—was there ever really a time he was so eager for relationship?

Parents always tell their kids, "It's hard to remember what it was like before you were born!" And that's been true with all five of mine. But when it comes to Jack, it goes further: I can't remember what it was like before the fog came. All I have are vague impressions that feel like dreams.

I remember he was an easy baby—far easier than his sisters had been. Our friends would marvel at how "chill" he was when we carried him into restaurants. And I remember he loved technology even then. When my girls had their first ballet recital, he sat on my lap in the pitch-dark auditorium, quiet and content with my glowing click wheel iPod.

As far as concrete memories, however, I'm ashamed to say I have only one that really sticks out. It involves my younger brother, whom my kids affectionately refer to as "Uncle Nay."

Uncle Nay used to come over and play with Jack all the time. He would toss him high enough into the air to make Sara wince, but the boy loved it. Jack would laugh with his whole body. And then the uncle would put him down and lift his own arms, yelling, "Touchdown!" The baby nephew would beam and lift his own arms in perfect mimicry.

One afternoon, Jack saw his uncle passing behind our house and got excited. He ran to the back entrance and pressed his face into the plastic doggy door and called out to him, "Tuh-down!"

That's the memory. I don't think it stuck with me just because it made us laugh, although it did that. No, it was the relationship. The word *touchdown* signified the connection between them. It was a real, give-and-take, uncle-to-nephew understanding.

We shared it, too, Jack and I, but the only reason I can say that today with any conviction is because I see the proof in the clip of him learning to walk. We shared moments like a typical father and son, and my heart ached when those moments went away. When the fog hit him, it hit me, too, and it expanded outward through time and space. It dimmed both my hopes for Jack's future and the way I see our shared past. I thank God for that video.

I can't tell you when clouds came and the fog set in, but I know before it did, everything was fine. Jackson had no problem speaking or relating, and he was hitting most of his developmental markers without any trouble for his first eighteen months. He was happy and active. He was awake and alert. My projector was clicking along, and the future was alive with possibilities.

Around that time, we moved the family from sub-urban East Texas to a place that felt to me like the end of the world—a community in the far, forgotten reaches of Northern California where the redwoods meet the sea. We were helping launch a new ministry on a property that used to be a hippie commune and now reminds people of Tolkien's Shire. It is a difficult setting in its remoteness, but for children, it is a wonderland.

There were trails through the hillside forest, pastures adorned with mysterious old sheds, and treasure-laden cabins hiding in the nooks of the ridge. On a clear day, you could see the blue haze of the mighty Pacific, just three miles down the old country road.

Horses and sheep and wild turkeys lived there, and the deer would come out of the forest every day to eat apples straight off the trees. If you wanted to, you could spy on them from your perch in one of the world's most unique tree forts, built into an old-growth redwood stump. Someone had cut those giants down a hundred years back—a puzzle and a shame—but the stumps continue to cast a spell of adventure on the land, or the Lord's Land, as it is now called.

That unique setting was what kept me from notic-ing Jack's regression. Like everyone else, he preferred the land outside to the cabin inside, and when he stepped out onto the wet grass, he would walk and walk and keep on walking. He might ignore our calls to "come see this baby deer," feet still shuffling forward, but we shrugged it off. Just Jack being Jack. Probably looking at some other wonder behind the deer. He was so independent. So chill.

It wasn't until well after he had turned two that I saw it. Sara was pregnant again at the time, and we had been in California for an entire year. That's when my friend Nathan made an offhand comment that was meant to be harmless: "You know, I don't think I've ever actually made eye contact with Jack."

The observation puzzled me at first. Really? Could it be true? Was Jack becoming distant? I thought it over and became further unsettled. He wasn't becoming distant—he had already been distant for months. He wasn't just avoiding Nathan's eyes; he was avoiding everyone's eyes.

Soon the comment began haunting me. The age of two is supposed to be a year of giant gains for typical children. They discover new things every day—new words, new joys, new powers—and they revel in those discoveries. But Jack's toddler curiosity had utterly vanished. He wasn't speaking, wasn't relating, wasn't even playing with his toys anymore. Instead, he was opting for kitchen utensils—spatulas especially. We had joked about that early on, but suddenly it wasn't funny anymore. Why wasn't he playing with his toys? Why had he stopped learning? Where had his language gone? "Touchdown, Jack!" we would say, raising our arms. He would just turn his head away.

Most of us take eye contact for granted. It's such an

easy reflex that we can't imagine how precious it really
is. But if the eyes are windows to the soul, then what is
eye contact except the bridge between souls? Even before
sounds can ever form themselves into words, and words
into sentences and sentences into sentiments, eye contact
is the primary medium of interpersonal understanding.
For a dad and his two-year-old mini-me, it is the bridge to
relationship itself.

Losing that bridge was catastrophic to me. It was the
first stab of the knife, and the cut went deeper than I could
have ever thought possible. I was too immature at that time
to think beyond that one form of connection. All I knew
was it hurt. A sharp pain and panic grew from that wound,
and it has yet to fully heal.

We didn't know much about autism then, but people
began whispering the word. We did a little research, but
since we didn't see all the symptoms we read about, we
dismissed the possibility. Routines were supposed to be a
big deal for autistic children, but Jack had no routine and
didn't seem to need one. Autistic kids were supposed to
stim—that is, to self-stimulate with obsessive activities like
spinning or jumping or hand flapping—but Jack wasn't
doing any of that.

Rather, he would float around our cabin, spatula in
hand, mumbling through vague melodies of worship
songs that played through a small speaker on the kitchen
windowsill. We had become incorporeal—the ghosts
through which he roamed day after day, week after week.

"What are you singing, there, Jack?"

No answer.

"Please, buddy, look here. Look at Daddy." I would turn his chin in my direction, but his eyes rebelled.

Sara and I decided he was fine, so "He's just a late bloomer" became our little mantra. He would come around. Besides, there was that one article about a kid who didn't talk till he was four and is now a biophysicist or something.

It was my own praying mother who put a crack in my defenses. She did it in an email that cut straight to the issue:

"Jason, I think Jack has autism and you are in denial."

I laughed at the words, thus proving her point. In my heart, I think I knew already.

∾

Denial comes in different shades. Sometimes people in denial simply pretend a thing isn't happening. That's the obvious kind. But there is a subtler and more common type that deals not so much in fantasy as in small adjustments of focus. All that's required is a slight rotation of the lens. What are we looking at? The crisis? Not anymore. Yes, yes, of course we see the crisis, but it's thrown out of focus now, and our eye is drawn toward this other puzzle over here. Any puzzle will do, provided it's easier to fix than the big one.

There is a stereotype about men being fixers, and I wish I could opt out of it. No one has ever asked me to fix a broken window or replace a timing belt. People know my well-earned reputation for being terrible with my hands. I don't fix things; I have friends who fix things.

And yet the generalization stands, even for me. Not all men fix cars, but pretty much the whole lot of us seek resolution. It is our go-to move. Our kids come to us with a problem, and our mind goes into search mode, scanning for simple answers.

"You're sad because you spilled your juice? Well, just wipe it up and get some more."

"You got a D on your math test? Well, see if you can take it again."

"Your friend hit you? Well, hit them back. No—wait! Talk to your teacher."

The operative word here is *well*. We want it all to go well. We want it all to be well. And in these contexts, the word gives off a vibe of irritation, as if the existence of the problem is, in itself, an annoyance, an offense that now needs a quick remedy. *Well* is a reflex. A counterstrike.

"You're crying? Well, grab a tissue, then!"

Bam.

But what happens when *well* has no place to punch? What if the problem is too big to fix with our carefully curated tactical wisdom?

"There's been a car accident."

"I want a divorce."

"Your son has autism."

Men like me flounder in the face of such grim realities. All our wells run dry.

We have to do something, then. Sure, we could take a hard, honest look at the situation, but that would mean facing our own inadequacies, which can be humiliating. What we need is an easy win. So we look for a new puzzle. A new quest.

There's a story of an Old Testament leper who did that very thing. Naaman of Syria was a powerful general who found his newly acquired leprosy to be a great inconvenience, so he sought help from Elisha, the mystic holy man from the south. When the general arrived at the prophet's home, he was met by a hired hand who gave him simple instructions: If Naaman wanted to be cured, he had to wash himself in the Jordan River seven times.

The general threw himself on his horse and rode off in disgust, ignoring the prophet's orders. It was a dismissive kind of task, and far too lowly a prescription. It certainly wasn't big enough to match the monster he faced. The Jordan was too foul for a man such as Naaman. There were crystal-clear streams in his own homeland that were more suitable. To bathe himself in the stench of the Jordan would be to face his own uncleanliness. His own rot.

Then, on his way out of town, one of his servants caught his ear: "My father, if the prophet had told you to do something great, would you not have done it? How much more then, when he says to you, 'Wash, and be clean'?" (2 Kings 5:13).

The servant knew his master well. Namaan was an adventurer in search of a solution as big as he was.

Adventurers go on great quests. They fight dragons, they hunt for grails, and they sail the seas to find the Golden Fleece. They win glory, and all their problems go away.

"But you've been given an easier cure," the servant was saying. "Far easier than questing." But he was wrong. Elisha's cure was simpler, more obvious, and more intelligent, but it wasn't easier.

Some would rather invent new dragons than face current pains. Take the executive with the broken marriage. Instead of pursuing his wife, he pursues the big merger, as if a thriving business had ever healed a throbbing home. Or consider the millennial graduate grappling for understanding of her own purpose. She knows she cannot find it in digital popularity, but there she is, living to impress her hundreds of faceless followers. All the while, the emptiness grows.

Each of these, and millions more, rotate their lenses to avoid investigating pains they already feel or truths they already know. This was the brand of denial I chose. When the realities of Jack's developmental problems settled in on me, I found my quest. I shifted my focus away from my son and toward something else: my own destiny. My "calling."

In hindsight, this focus shift was a predictable pivot. Growing up, I always did have an overinflated view of my own importance in the Kingdom of God. People used to tell me I would be a powerful preacher. A twenty-first-century John Wesley or Charles Finney. My friends and I had plans to travel and preach and pray, and it was going to be amazing. We would be a big deal together, and I would be in the middle of the action, using my words. My powerful words.

Now, though, at this fledgling ministry in the middle of what suddenly seemed like a dark fairy tale, my work felt downright menial. I was sitting through long meetings, cleaning dusty cabins, and chopping endless piles of wood. All of it was noble and necessary work, I knew, but where was the stage? Where was the microphone? The clock was ticking. I was turning thirty, and I had yet to start a single revival!

I didn't have to put myself through that. I could have just entered the Jordan and faced my pain. But I wasn't strong enough, so I diverted my own attention from Jack's obvious drift into autism by leaning into my own early midlife crisis. And against all odds, I succeeded. Just a slight focus adjustment was all it took. The boy looked blurry now, but I stood front and center in a clear, sepia-tone landscape: a passionate young man ready to sail the seven seas in search of his fate.

If I could have seen my true self, I might have seen a far different image. I was a bleary-eyed boy standing in an emergency room, holding a clipboard, and puzzling over the first question: "What is your name?"

And isn't that what we're really doing at such times? Aren't we just grappling over our own identities? Any problem big enough to run away from is probably threatening us there, in that tender spot. The mirror of our soul. Are we still important enough, even in our fear? Can we still contribute? Because we are exposed now. Weak and thin and babbling.

We were strong once. Can we be strong again? We are broken. *Please, God, for your sake and the sake of your Kingdom, tell us how to be healed. Please, tell us how you see us.*

I had already been thinking over all this for months when our ministry invited a speaker to come guide us through a day of silence and solitude. It would be a targeted time to hear God's voice. This was my first experience with the ancient brand of guided spiritual direction. I had grown up with the louder kind, so this calm pursuit of orthodox spiritual discipline felt strangely novel.

When the day finally came, the teacher handed us a pamphlet full of prayers with various Scriptures and instructions on what to discuss with God. One of his prescriptions seemed odd and contrived to me. He told us to go to a quiet place and sit down next to an empty seat, imagining Christ himself sitting there with us. Then, he said, we should talk to that empty seat, because God would be, in reality, right there listening.

I went to the best place I knew of: the beautiful and secluded Navarro Beach, where a river reservoirs during the summer but always finds a way to break through to the ocean when the rains come. The crescent stretch of sand reshapes itself every year between the cliff on the north end and the outcropping of giant rocks to the south. I found a place for both Jesus and me on one of those southern boulders, and we sat up there watching the ocean pound the shoreline.

Then we talked.

I told him my fears about Jack. I told him of my

questions about my future. I told him of my frustrations at feeling lost. All of it he knew already, and yet it felt fresh, as if we were discussing it for the first time.

Finally, I came to the question that now burned hottest under my skin. It was the same question that Jesus had once asked his own friend: "Who do you say that I am?" (Matthew 16:15, NASB).

I'm sad to say that even in that moment, I craved both affirmation and diversion, destiny and denial. Thus, I didn't deserve an answer. But God rarely gives us what we actually deserve. People say he is not fair, and they are right. He is far too kind to be fair.

That morning, he answered me in spite of myself. His words crashed into my heart in the loudest inaudible whisper I have ever heard:

"You are my son."

Then, before the wind even had a chance to whip the tears away from my face, I remembered the words of a song Jack had been mumbling. It was a modern snippet from the ancient Song of Solomon: "You have ravished my heart / With one glance of your eye"![1]

I thought of Jack. I thought of the thrill that filled me in those rare moments when he looked at me. He was my son. My delight. And he had no idea how much he meant to me. Neither, it seemed, did I have any notion of my Father's love.

Weeping took me then. Tears of relief and of resolve. At last I understood how to drop anchor there at the beginning of the long storm. I couldn't secure myself in the seabed of personal identity, for my own sense of self was loose and shallow. My passions were ever morphing and conflicted, and even my healthiest desires waxed and waned like the Pacific tides. True identity is not something we ourselves can claim, no matter what our favorite Disney movies say. Identity, like life itself, has to be a gift from someone else. And the only reliable giver is our Father, who begot us.

This was not some new special revelation only for me. The Scriptures are full of parental imagery. God rejoices over us "with shouts of joy" (Zephaniah 3:17, NASB). He pulls us close to him and hides us in the shadow of his wings (see Psalm 17:8). And even when we smell like swine, he runs headlong to welcome us home (see Luke 15:11-20). He is more than just our Father; he is our Dad (see Romans 8:15). Before we ever became teachers or writers or electricians or web developers, we were his kids. Our identities begin and end with the Alpha and Omega. Visions, vocations, and occupations are all subservient to that core; they are merely hats we wear for seasonal assignments.

Who are we, really? We are his kids.

Thus, God's answer proved a double grace, calming not only my identity as a son but also my fears as a father. If God adored me the way that I already adored my own son, it meant I could stop readjusting my lens. I could, at last, look my crisis full in the face and say the words I despaired to say: *My son has autism, and my life might never be the same.* I was weak, but the storm would not overtake me—not while I sat on the Rock Immovable.

All this is just as true for you as it was for me. None of us can live for long in denial, milling about with name tags and quests for diversion. Eventually, we will have to acknowledge the humbling truths around us:

This thing we are facing is real.

We cannot fix it.

We cannot make everything well.

We cannot even guarantee a positive outcome.

Our lives might, indeed, be changed forever.

It feels grim, I know, and we would all despair if we faced these truths alone. But this is precisely why we must find ourselves in our Lord. We are not alone. We are hemmed in by warm divinity: "Christ with me, Christ before me, Christ behind me, Christ in me."[2] Only in the arms of our loving Father will we find the strength to stand, to weep, and to walk this journey. The road might be a long one, but eventually, because of his unrelenting grace, we will find a table set before us even there, in the presence of our enemies (see Psalm 23:5). A feast prepared by our Father, and an empty chair.

Maybe you rushed past it before. Maybe you tried to face the gathering storm without ever being anchored to your Dad. If you did, let me encourage you: Begin again, this time by sitting. Climb on the Rock, friend, and let him speak your name.

CHAPTER 3

Psalms of Lament

WE HOLD TO a curious religious decorum in the Western church. We believe that God is omniscient, and yet we try to hide the truth from him out of Christian propriety. We bury whatever distasteful thing lurks inside us out of a sense of respect. One might even call it upward condescension. As if the Omnipotent were fragile. As if the Rock of Ages, who juggles galaxies with his fingertips, must be sheltered from the facts.

I've seen this phenomenon in some charismatic environments, where parents refuse to say the name of even seasonal ailments their children bring home from school. "Don't speak it out," they say, as if a token acknowledgment of the snot dripping from their kids' noses would give power to the cold, thus tying God's hands behind his back. It is an ironic quirk for a people marked with such high belief in God's power.

I've seen it in subtler ways, too, like our cliché family battles that erupt a half hour before church. These skirmishes over collared shirts and ironed pants can get heated, but they tend to wind down just as we step onto the church parking lot. Why the quick cease-fire? Because we're entering God's house, and we need to be perfect toy soldiers. For we all know, he looketh not on the inward appearance but on the whiteness of our teeth.

When my daughters were young, they used to hide under a blanket and call me to find them. I would oblige them, lumbering around the room, pretending not to see the two laughing forms underneath the blanket in the center of the carpet. "Where are they?" I would ask with feigned befuddlement. "I can't find them, Sara. Maybe I'll just sit on this blanket and think about it!" And the laughter would erupt as they fled the weight of the giant.

If you don't mind my saying so, this is how I imagine it looks when we try to hide from the perfect eye of our Creator. It's childish and a little embarrassing. God sees reality exactly how it exists, and nothing escapes his gaze—neither snotty noses nor starched hypocrisy—and yet we persist in hiding from him. We especially do it when we are angry with God.

I wasn't angry at first. God had reassured me of his care,

and that protected me from some poisonous mind-sets. For instance, I never saw Jack's autism as a punishment for something we did. The picture of an angry Thor swinging his vengeful hammer at unsuspecting unfortunates was far from me. I couldn't make it stick even when I felt sorry for myself. How could I ever see God like that when he was my Father? He cared for my family. He was for us.

But when the full force of the storm hit, my disappointment turned to fear, and my fear into rage. I had to decide what to do with that rage.

Fortunately, Sara and I didn't have to walk through any of it on our own. The growing Hague household had made the cross-country move to the Shire with three dear friends, and my story cannot move forward unless I describe them to you. There was Janae, the show-tune-singing Californian who had disguised herself as a southern belle. Janae played dual roles as our greatest encourager and our kids' personal Mary Poppins.

And then there were George and Karen, one of the unlikeliest couples that ever was. George grew up half naked in the jungles of Papua New Guinea, and he came to America as a young man to be trained as a Christian missionary. "George of the Jungle," as we called him, was renowned for many great exploits in the States, not the least of which was eating spiders for shock value and turning any ballad into reggae on his guitar. He might be the single most likable human being I have ever known.

One of the very few who could rival that title was his

own wife. Karen was a native Idahoan who shunned the spotlight George so reveled in. There was never anything quite so entertaining as watching Karen roll her eyes while her husband charmed the Sam's Club employees into giving him extra free samples. Her smile was soft and warm—the kind of smile that made strangers stop her on the street and entrust her with their deepest pains. And she herself, a two-time cancer survivor, knew all about deep pains. She could release a knowing, confident peace with that smile.

The five of us had worked together for years with our missions agency, but our relationship wasn't really about ministry. It was about being a family. These guys had become an uncle and aunties to our children. Life was about watching season after season of *24* together. It was about George making Janae laugh way too loudly after the kids had gone to bed. It was about Karen making silly faces with my kids on the Photo Booth app. It was about breaking bread and singing spontaneous songs both of silliness and of worship. It was about celebrating life. Especially new life.

When Sara delivered our fourth child, just one month after God answered me on the beach, there was much celebration in our little crew. We even forgot about the troubles with Jack for a few days. Samuel was a big and beautiful baby, and we all rejoiced at the fact that the Hague clan was now even: two boys and two girls. The whole family, including the two aunties and one uncle, rejoiced together.

A week later, a stethoscope put an end to the

celebration. Samuel's heart didn't thud like a newborn's
heart ought to. It made a swishing sound, like a bad Darth
Vader impression.

The doctor sent us down to see a cardiologist in San
Francisco, a three-hour drive. There was a long test in a
dark room with a woman who looked like she was doing an
ultrasound on his chest. It was an echocardiagram, techni-
cally, and she was looking at the chambers of his heart. Her
face displayed no emotion as she moved her instrument
back and forth across his chest, then hit a few keys to cap-
ture image after warped, disorienting, color-shifting image.

The cardiologist called us into his office a half hour
later. It was a big room with a massive window overlooking
Golden Gate Park and the magnificent bay behind. I stared
out the window, my hands gripping the back of the leather
chair in front of the man's imposing desk.

"Why don't you guys sit down," he said, motioning to
the chair. Sara sat. I didn't. I kept staring.

The white-haired man spoke again, this time a little
softer. "You should sit down."

I knew what that moment was. I knew it so well, for it
was one I had tried my best to edit out of my precious daydreams. It was a definitive moment, like the one I had been
hoping to avoid with Jack—the moment of a knowing,
can't-pretend-anymore diagnosis. Jack's had been a gradual,
sinking truth that had still not fully settled. This moment
was different. It hit me like a felled redwood giant, and I
was powerless to avoid it, just as I was powerless to silence

the knowing taunts of my dark daydreams that now screamed, *This is what crisis feels like!*

Sam had a hole between the chambers of his heart, and one of his valves was severely deformed. This presented a dangerous problem: His heart was pumping blood with too little oxygen. It was a serious condition that could be repaired only through open-heart surgery. But since open-heart surgery was so much more dangerous for newborns, the cardiologist wanted to buy some time, and he sent us home with a list of instructions:

> This child was not allowed to cry. If he cried too much, he might run out of oxygen, turn blue, and pass out, with potentially catastrophic effects.
>
> This child was not allowed to get sick. Yes, yes, winter was almost upon us, and winters in that region are cold and wet, but if he got sick, his heart could get too distressed.
>
> This child was not allowed to be around other people, because other people bring their own sicknesses with them.

It was an absurd list. We were experienced parents by then, and we knew two ironclad truths about babies: They will cry, and they will get sick.

We hardly spoke on that three-hour drive home. The concoction of shock and fear and confusion was thick. First Jack's impending diagnosis, and now this.

At home, we at once became intently aware of our boy's

breathing. Any whiff of whimpering set us into a small panic. *Pick him up. Make him stop. Make him happy. Don't let him cry. Shhhh . . . shhhh . . .* The girls would go stark silent in those moments, hoisting their tiny prayers for their newborn brother, and Jack would go on doing what he always did: playing with his spatulas and humming the melody, "How great is our God . . . Sing with me, how great is our God . . ."

That hopeful anthem was out of place in our kitchen. We knew God was good, but he didn't feel great to us. Not right then. I remember sinking into a callous self-pity under the weight of my double crisis. "One boy born with a broken mind," I lamented, "and one with a broken heart."

But as I said, we were surrounded by family, so I couldn't sink too far. Janae soothed us with the giant hugs for which she is so famous, and George and Karen did their best to keep us laughing. And God was still there, of course. We didn't understand what he was doing, but we knew we were not alone. We would get through this. Somehow.

Then, one bright afternoon, I stepped onto the rocky path toward our ministry office, and Karen was walking toward me, her black curly hair hanging free in all directions like always. But something was different this time. Her face was less placid than usual.

"Jason, I need to talk to you." Her expression was careful. Apologetic.

"What's the matter?" I was on edge now.

She took a deep breath. "I found a lump."

I felt faint. My head drifted away from her. "No. No . . ."

"Listen," she said, stepping toward me. She could sense my panic rising. "Listen. We're going to get through this. This isn't our first rodeo."

It was true. She had beaten leukemia when she was seventeen, then fought off breast cancer at thirty-two. By then, she and George were full of faith, and her peace was genuine. We soon discovered, however, that those earlier battles had taken a great toll on her body. A person can only handle so much radiation poisoning over her lifetime. Karen's body had already taken all it could bear. This time, the doctors could not offer much help or hope. All we could do was pray.

Prayer used to feel like a power option. Now it was a meager last resort.

It wasn't George and Karen's first rodeo, but it was mine. Thirty years of life unstained by serious hardship, and now in three months, three blows. First my sons, now my sister.

My memories blur together after that. There were meetings and cold rains and blank stares, stacks of firewood, and piles of unspoken fears. How long they went unspoken, I can't say. It could have been days or weeks, but I remember the slow churning in my gut that so often accompanies quiet resentment.

In essence, I gave God the silent treatment. But if I thought there was any power in it, I was wrong. It only made the pain more acute. The human mouth is, among other things, an effective pressure-release valve. Keep it closed too long, and the burning beneath will become

unbearable. It's true of human relationships, and it's also
true of prayer. Even David the psalmist, the author of the
church's most enduring prayer book, attempted to give God
the cold shoulder once, and it didn't work for him either:

> I was mute and silent;
>> I held my peace to no avail,
> and my distress grew worse.
>> My heart became hot within me.
> As I mused, the fire burned;
>> then I spoke with my tongue.
>
> PSALM 39:2-3, ESV

When he couldn't bear it any longer, he finally did speak.
The rest of his psalm is a blaze of confession, accusation,
and distress. David was renowned for his fire, and he never
could hold it in for very long. Passion—sometimes for battle,
sometimes for women, sometimes for God—permeated him.
When the Ark of the Covenant was brought to Jerusalem, he
danced in his skivvies. When his would-be murderer died,
he wept openly. When his enemies threatened him, he tried
to pray down lightning. And when he felt abandoned by
God, he turned his head to the sky and screamed,

> Why are You so far from helping Me,
> And from the words of My groaning?
> O My God, I cry in the daytime, but You do not hear.
>
> PSALM 22:1-2

We don't like such psalms nowadays. We often skip past compositions like these in favor of greener pastures. These psalms are too dark. Too Old Testament.

That's not the main reason we shy away from them, though, and we know it. The real reason is our religious decorum—our inexplicable thirst to hide our faces from our Creator. It is one thing to finally face the pains inside ourselves; it is another thing entirely to bring those pains to the altar of confession. Just who do we think we are, anyway? Who did David think he was, shoving his fist into the sky like that? Nobody wants to hear him say to God,

> Attend to me, and hear me;
> I am restless in my complaint, and moan noisily.
>
> PSALM 55:2

We want the safe shepherd boy, the cute little slinger who sometimes played the harp for the grown-ups. Give us the praise anthems of the poet, the lover, the slayer of giants, and let us sing verse, chorus, verse, chorus, and bridge. Then we'll change keys and sing the chorus again, this time with more feeling. The mainliners will nod gravely, the evangelicals will sway, and the charismatics will two-step in the aisles, because the psalms of praise belong to all of us. As for the desolate prayers, we have no affinity with them.

The Bible's songbook, however, is littered with enough of these sentiments to make us all blush. We cannot ignore them. These are not sanitized sonnets for Sunday; these are poems that bleed.

David wasn't the only one who wrote such scandalous stanzas either. His fellow songwriters, the Sons of Korah, gave us this line:

Awake! Why do You sleep, O Lord?
Arise! Do not cast us off forever.
Why do You hide Your face,
And forget our affliction and our oppression?
PSALM 44:23-24

And Job, after he had lost everything, lashed out at God in an even more striking way:

Will You never turn Your gaze away from me,
Nor let me alone until I swallow my spittle?
Have I sinned? What have I done to You,
O watcher of men?
Why have You set me as Your target,
So that I am a burden to myself?
JOB 7:19-20, NASB

My own complaint didn't go so far as Job's. Not only was his crisis many times heavier than mine, but I also didn't actually believe God was targeting me—how could I after his whispers about my sonship? And yet in one sense, that was part of the problem. If he was my Father who only wanted the best for me, why wasn't he stepping in? It made no sense. He had all the power in the universe, but he wouldn't wield it.

Why doesn't he step in? Isn't that the question we're all asking? Is it because he can't, or because he won't? After that, the accusations cascade:

Don't you see me, Jesus?
Can't you tell I'm hurting?
Why me? Why now?
What have I done wrong?

For my part, I thought I had been more or less obedient to God. I had followed the path he laid out for me. I had dedicated my life to explaining and defending his goodness. And yet here I was, forgotten and out of favor, feeling a bit like Jeremiah at his angriest:

You pushed me into this, GOD, and I let you do it. . . . And now I'm a public joke.

JEREMIAH 20:7, MSG

The frustrations are already there inside us, see. The doubts and disappointments, the accusations against God often lie in wait, covered in platitudes and postured peace. We know they are there, but we tell ourselves that it's all right. Such thoughts are out-of-bounds, but as long as we can smother them with enough *Praise the Lord*s, they are harmless. We are wrong, though. These hanging questions are tumors feasting on our nerves and poisoning our trust.

This is the tragedy of our curious decorum. We think we are being respectful. We think God will hear our hearts' cries if only we can sanitize them. But in the act of sanitization, we prove we do not trust him, as if he could only handle the sugar-coated prayers.

Thus, we hide our faces behind veils to protect our Savior from the ugly, muddy truth of our souls, and in doing so we defer intimacy until the next life. Only in the great by-and-by, when our sharp edges are dull enough and our fires have sufficiently cooled, can we let him hear the full and unedited truth—the same truth he's seen lying in our hearts since the day we learned to feel.

I'm not advocating transparency for its own sake. I'm advocating transparency as a first step toward spiritual healing. If we've come to terms with our broken places, we do not have to hide them from God. In fact, we must not.

Honesty with God is not only a better policy than hiding but is also, I believe, more biblical. God's best friends, after all, seemed to be the most blunt in prayer. David, Job, and Jeremiah we've already mentioned. But didn't Abraham himself haggle over the destruction of Sodom? And didn't the law giver Moses do the same over Israel? Didn't Jacob face off against God in a midnight wrestling match?[1] Part of what made the heroes of the faith heroes was the boldness they displayed before a powerful and often terrifying God.

If that isn't enough, consider this: Jesus himself prayed exactly this way. While hanging on the cross, he cried out to his Father with the words of one of David's most brutal, honest psalms:

> My God, My God, why have You forsaken Me?
> MATTHEW 27:46; SEE ALSO PSALM 22:1

Yes, in the Land of Unanswered Prayer, we must follow Christ even in this way. That is why David urged us, "Cast your burden on the LORD, and He shall sustain you" (Psalm 55:22).

Cast it. Hurl it. Chuck it. Don't hide it, and don't lay it there delicately. God is not a child in need of sheltering. So give it to him, however seemingly toxic. It will feel audacious and improper to address a King this way. But you are not some random peasant; you are his son or his daughter. His beloved. So take aim, friend.

Tell him the truth.

After letting my own questions fester for a time, I found myself driving back to Navarro Beach, my personal thin place between earth and heaven. The landscape was empty that day. The sky looked empty too. But he was up there, somewhere.

Back and forth across the sands I marched, fists clutching and blood pumping. I fumed, and the Pacific waters fumed with me. This wasn't a day for whispers, so I didn't crawl up on the rock. I didn't imagine myself having tea with Jesus. No. To everything there is a season: a time for peace and a time for war; hours for whispers and hours for screams.

I let him have it. I screamed that it was all wrong. My sons didn't deserve this. My friends Karen and George didn't deserve this. What, was he going to tease me now? I had even been taking new steps of faith in his power to heal in supernatural ways. Was this his way of rewarding me? Was this some kind of sick Abrahamic test? Because I thought I'd already been faithful. What else did he want from me?

On and on I raged like an injured soldier, pointing at the wounds caused by a shrapnel grenade. I didn't want those wounds. But they were there. "Can't you see what's happening to me?"

Finally, I ran out of steam, and my cursing mouth fell silent. The gray clouds continued to drift silently overhead. There was no crack of thunder, no bolt of blue lightning. Nothing.

But there was a change inside me, and I felt it almost at once. I felt the presence of a crying Spirit drawing near to me. He had known my pains already, because he shared them. But only now that I acknowledged them could he begin his work of comfort in earnest.

My psalm of lament ended almost as quickly as it had begun. My anger burned hot and then was gone. An hour later, I sat sunken in a sofa, and my remaining tears poured out in sadness, not rage. My friend Nathan sat with me. He was the one who had first recognized something wasn't quite right with Jack. Over the previous eighteen months, he had become not only a friend but also something like a personal sage—older, wiser, and gentler than me.

I prayed aloud through my tears. "You've got to heal at least one of them, Lord. Please." I was pleading now. Bargaining. "You've got to show me you have the power. Heal just one."

Nathan put his hand on my shoulder and joined my prayer with those ancient words the Lord spoke through Isaiah: "Lord, show Jason the treasures in the dark."[2]

Little did I realize I had just discovered the first treasure: Honesty with God is the beginning of healing. We might be dead wrong in the particulars of our accusations, but that isn't the point. Very often, it's not the substance of our buried objections that keep God at arm's length, but the fact that we have buried objections in the first place. We must come out of our hiding places.

I suspect this is why David's psalms of lament so often swing to thanksgiving at the end. As long as he sat mute, his wounds oozed and festered. But when he admitted his pains, he bid the Healer come close. He trusted his Shepherd, and that made all the difference.

It was true for the psalmist, and it is true for all of us, whatever our wounds. Christ does not shrink back from lepers. He touches them.

CHAPTER 4

The Forgetting Place

GRIEF RARELY WALKS IN A STRAIGHT LINE. For me,
it meandered. My breakthrough moments on the beach,
as potent as they were, did not usher me swiftly into the
realm of blissful acceptance. Rather, those were important,
incremental steps toward wholeness. I needed to know
God would never leave me. I needed to invite him into my
anger and confusion.

When those questions settled in my spirit, I was able to
move forward. But make no mistake, the way forward was
long and arduous. It is now a well-worn path.

Psychologists have talked for years about the stages of
grief. These stages don't show up only after funerals. We
grieve for many reasons: for the death of our loved ones, yes,

but also for broken relationships, for connections we cannot seem to make, and for tomorrows we can no longer count on. In describing my own journey, I am by no means comparing my scars with the scars of those who have lost family members. They are not the same. I didn't lose my son. I'll be honest, though—at the time, it sure felt like I had. "Everybody hurts," as the song goes.[1] And no matter how it is that we come to hurt, most of us seem to walk through denial, anger, bargaining, depression, and acceptance.

I had moved long past denial by this time, and my anger cooled quickly after my psalm of lament. Bargaining, too, was a short phase marked by my plea with God to "heal just one." All of those came and went even before Jack's formal diagnosis. He was three years old. That's when the fourth stage settled in on me: depression.

When I think of the depression years, I think of the drive to Jack's special school in Eugene, Oregon. We had made the move from California the week following his diagnosis. Why did we leave? Because of this early-education program we enrolled him in. Or because we needed to be closer to civilization. Or because our feet itched, as feet in crisis are wont to do.

Thankfully, one of our three crises had cooled. Samuel did not receive a divine, sudden healing, but he did grow big enough and healthy enough to undergo open-heart surgery at six months of age, and the procedure had been a success. His prognosis was still somewhat questionable. We didn't know, for instance, what restrictions he might end up having on physical exertion down the road, and we knew he would have to see cardiologists for the rest of his life. Those cardiologists, they said, would have to monitor his leaky valve and schedule further surgeries every five to ten years.

I would think about all of it while I drove. I would think about how even though one troubled spot in our own hearts had settled, we didn't have any peace regarding Jack's situation.

It was a twenty-seven-minute drive from our house in the country to the special school in the university district. Jack would sit behind me in our '90s minivan, staring through the wide, tinted windows. He was either taking all of it in or none of it—I still don't know which. I would lean back and stretch to tickle him with my right arm, and he almost never responded. So I would sigh and plug an earbud into my skull to flush out the silence with my noise of choice: sports podcasts.

Four days a week, I drove him through the lush Willamette Valley, past sheep in green pastures next to still waters, but I could not bring myself to sing any psalms of contentment. The valley, shallow as it was, made me feel more claustrophobic than peaceful. The Coburg hills hemmed me in on the left side, the coastal mountains on the right, and our low ceiling of clouds leaked incessantly.

The university district was always bustling. Light water sprays would leap up from beneath the tires of small hybrid vehicles and coat my windshield with a thin blur, making it hard to read the assortment of political bumper stickers from last semester's causes. Those students were always running out of space on their cars to be angry, but at least they could actually feel things. I envied them for that.

We would find a parking space in the front of a wide, brick building full of experts and therapists and grad students working in gated classrooms full of clipboards and sensory toys. We were lucky to get him into the program. Really lucky. Even then, I knew I should feel thankful.

"We're here, Jack."

It was a stately building, this special school, with deep red bricks and a big, round silver button at the entrance— you know the kind, marked with a blue stick figure sitting in the outline of a wheelchair. Jack liked to push it and let the door swing open on its own. Some days, though, I would push the door open myself. I didn't like that button.

The hallway was wide, dim, and full of echoes. We would pass the first door, then the second, and finally stop at the familiar inlet. There was a closed sliding gate of prison bars just outside the cubbyholes. Three- and four-year-old children were there, slipping backpacks off shoulders, matching pictures to hooks so they could hang their coats in the appropriate places.

"Good morning, Jack!" a kind woman with beaming eyes would say. She liked him. I could tell she wasn't pretending. That was nice.

"Say good morning, bud," I would prompt, because that was the script. But he wouldn't follow it.

We would slide open the prison bars, and I would give her the scoop: Jack had been up since probably two for no apparent reason, so she shouldn't except much from him. She would give a vigorous nod of understanding. She knew the drill, and she would do her best.

"Say good-bye to Dad, Jack!"

He wouldn't, so I would shrug and smile. It was okay. Really, it was totally fine. I would see him in three hours.

The hallway always felt dark and empty. Darker than when I came in, somehow. And no, I wouldn't push the cursed button on the way out either, thank you very much.

By the time my feet hit the pavement, the entire routine would begin to cave in on me. The whole thing was so wrong. So unfair. So unlike the life I had expected. So unlike my precious propaganda. I wasn't angry at God; he had heard my prayer and felt my pain. But he had not answered me, and my sorrow was as thick as the Oregon fog.

As I think about those drop-offs, I can still feel the river rising up inside me, wanting out. I remember the blinking, the rapid breathing, and the quick swallowing. I remember my hands grappling between the seats for my earbuds: my personal prescription. I needed the medicine they offered. I needed to return to a world where all that was at stake was a wild card berth or a free agency signing, or whether or not LeBron would leave the Cavaliers after the season.

I would find a coffee shop that wasn't overrun with undergrads—one with a free table next to open outlets. I had projects to work on. Any project would do.

A sip of dark roast, a quick log-in, and another hour of *The Dan Patrick Show*. That combination did the trick. I took in the medicine through my fingers, through my ears, through my cup until the numbness took over. This was not my happy place. No, it was my forgetting place. I went as often as I needed to.

Our forgetting places are all too easy to find in modern America. We are the land of irrepressible noise. It doesn't matter where we go; we can't escape it. As long as internet signals can animate our devices with their invisible cords, we are hostages. Our phones alone have reprogrammed our brains and latched on to our psyches, chaining them to the dopamine that accompanies each new notification, each opportunity for fresh stimuli.[2] Tapping and swiping are now compulsory behaviors that do nothing but serve our hunger for on-time information and on-fleek entertainment.

In this way, the engrossing noise emanating from our screens is our new international drug of choice. And just like the most illicit narcotics of our day, noise can prevent us from feeling pain.

I was a noise junkie by then. I needed its numbing effects. I needed to forget not just about Jack's drift but also about Karen's absence. We had lost her.

Cancer had ravaged Karen's body in nine months, finally nesting in her brain. In the early days of 2010, she went down with a massive seizure that landed her in the intensive care unit.

We packed up the van after that and met her family in California, where we lingered with them for days in the hospital, praying desperate prayers and trying to say comforting words. She couldn't speak at all by then. All she could do was nod while Janae pointed to letters on a whiteboard. In this way, she spelled out her good-byes.

I was in the room when she breathed her last. It's an image I cannot shake but would never trade: George cradling his wife in his arms, singing, "You are so beautiful to me." She was thirty-three.

But from my seat in the coffee shop, I didn't have to think about any of it. I didn't have to think about how much I missed her, or how much more George missed her. I didn't have to wonder why God didn't heal her even though thousands of people around the world prayed and some gave "prophetic" words indicating he would. We had believed them—she would not die. Just like how God had created my son for relationship, even though he couldn't experience it. Those accusations floated through me, half-formed and rarely realized.

My forgetting place extended to my couch at home. The projects went on and on. I was on my computer at all hours, and my earbuds were always in. My kids would try to play with me, but I was too busy. Sara urged me to engage with Jack, but with so little reciprocation, what was the point? Besides, I had stuff to do. There was noise to engage. And what fool would choose pain when there was medication so readily available?

George wasn't taking it, though. His native culture is different from ours. In his homeland of Papua New Guinea, pain is something you choose to feel. When someone died in his village, mourners would come from all over the highlands. There would be a special place for them: the crying house. For weeks, friends and family would weep day and night for the fallen. There were no Wi-Fi signals to anesthetize them, and no iPhones to distract them from the real business of grieving. They faced it.

A month after Karen died, George made a brief visit back to his village, and they mourned in exactly this way. His family set up a special tent for her, and they wept with him for hours on end.

When he came back, he brought the jungle with him. He floated from our couch to the neighbor's guest room for months. "Where's George?" people would ask. We would shrug. He was off somewhere with his guitar. Somewhere in the woods, probably. Somewhere choosing to ache, to talk to God, and to remember his wife.

While I continued to make my numb trips past the silver button and into my forgetting place, George seemed to be thriving. Don't get me wrong; he was hurting, obviously, but he was also at peace. A sense of calm clung to him. There was no angst. While I was actively avoiding my pains, he was embracing his own. And only one of us was finding anything like restoration.

How strange that we in the West confuse the lack of pain with wellness. As long as we aren't feeling any current discomfort, we assume everything is okay. Our strategy, then, is to find the right mix of medication to keep that discomfort at bay.

The problem, though, is that pain is never its own root. It is a symptom of a deeper cause. Whether in the body or in the heart, there is always a reason behind the thing that hurts. Pain is just the alarm that points to it, often urging us to take necessary action:

Your hand is on a burning surface! Remove it!

You just stepped on a nail! Take it out!

Your soul hurts. Your heart is bruised. Find out why.

We would do well to heed such alarms and not try so hard to avoid them. They are gifts. If you don't believe me, consider what happens to those who suffer nerve damage and lose the ability to send and receive pain signals. Far from being an escape, this condition presents a serious health crisis. Leprosy patients can do horrendous damage to their bodies quite by accident. Painless blisters and sores form on their extremities, and before the patient realizes it, those sores can get infected, with even more disastrous results.

It is a dangerous thing, then, to avoid our wounds or numb them too much. Our emotional wounds, like our physical injuries, can fester deep beneath the numbness. No amount of chemicals or diversions can keep us safe. We cannot chase away our brokenness with alcohol or pornography, with binge-watching or binge-working. Our blinking, buzzing, automatically updating noisemakers have no power to restore, only to distract. They promise us a path around the pain, but they lie. There is no way to circumvent the aches. We have to go toward them. We have to investigate them.

In my case, I already knew where the wound was. It lay at the intersection of my expectations and my new reality. Even though I understood now that life could never be as I had once hoped, I had never gotten down to the business of moving forward. While my wife was taking Jack by the hand and learning all she could about this thing called autism—its causes and treatments, the science and the stories—I sat on the bench with my own personal medications. I didn't want to know any of it.

As a result, I became cold and distant from all my children, not just Jack. I withdrew. Friends were there, but I did not access them. In fact, I didn't want to be around anybody—a strange shift for someone like me, who had always been an extrovert. I just wanted to be alone with my noise.

Nothing good came from running. Nothing ever does. No matter how far we travel, reality still waits for us back home. We can't prolong our return forever. Eventually, we all have to figure out how to accept truth. The only alternative is to drown ourselves in our addictions forever. We've all seen it happen, and it's the saddest thing in the world to watch sorrow reach its full measure.

No, escape isn't an option. We know we must face our struggles. So why do we run?

I'll tell you why I ran. I ran for the same reason people

avoid calling the doctor about those nagging dizzy spells or those strange growths on their neck. I was afraid.

There is no script for dealing with severe autism. In fact, one of the most common clichés in the special-needs community goes like this: "If you've met one child with autism, you've met one child with autism." The variance of behaviors is extreme, and the outlook for autistic children is diverse. Some figure out speech or social skills a little late but go on to live happy, productive lives. Others are strong in, say, science and math, but they struggle their entire lives to understand basic interaction with people around them. And still others may never figure out the mechanics of bowel control, let alone balancing a checkbook.

There were just too many uncertainties. Too many things to fear. But then, isn't that the nature of life in general? We're all dealing with special needs; that is, we all have needs, and they are all peculiar to our own situations. Life is an uncertain maze full of question marks, dead-ends, and other horrors. There are many, many things to fear.

But "perfect love casts out fear" (1 John 4:18). I wish I had taken God up on that promise. I wish I had grasped this truth: that the name of the Lord is a strong tower, and the righteous don't by any means run away from it. No, they run into it. And there, they are safe (see Proverbs 18:10).

George remembered it. He remembered at night especially, because that's when he needed to remember it the most. His tribe in Papua New Guinea still holds to heavy superstitions about the dark. They believe that spirits roam freely at night, especially following a death. In fact, oftentimes while the women go on wailing at night in the crying house, the men band together outside and keep watch over the grave for fear that some wayward spirit might steal away the body. Even though George had lived in America for more than twelve years and had become a Christian before that, he still grappled with an intense fear of the dark. If I had grown up in that kind of spiritual environment, seeing all the things he saw, I would no doubt have carried the same fear with me.

After Karen died, George did something he never thought he would do: He started walking at night. Up and down the rural Oregon roads, he walked after we had all gone to bed, and while he walked, he prayed and he cried tears into the void around him. When you're in the dark, there is no blinking light to steal away your thoughts or your pains. There is only the self and the empty sky.

George emptied himself out to the sky. He asked God all the *why?* questions, he sang praise in the midst of his tears, and he wept for his beloved, all while watching the trees lest some ghost of his homeland appear to steal away his sanity.

"I wanted to see if any of it was real," he told me later. "I wanted to see if there was anything to any of it: the spirits or even God. I felt lost. I had no idea what was going to happen."

And nothing did happen. God did not step out of the

bushes with a light and an elixir for wounded widowers. He did not explain why he had not healed Karen. The mystery remained, and George's heart throbbed in the crater where his wife had been. Mourning would go on hurting.

No, nothing happened there in the darkness except for this one thing: "The fear was gone," he said.

"Jason, I realized in the dark that I was surrounded by love. I knew I could have run away from God, but I understood that was stupid. I had seen too much of his goodness already. What I needed to do was run *to* him. To rest beneath the shadow of his wings."

That's what he did in the dark. He followed the example of Jesus, who had himself prayed alone in the dead of night. Jesus had shown his own grief to his Father—grief over his dear friend who had just rejected him, over the other betrayers who had rejected him, and over the terrible cup he was about to drink.

Yes, George followed his Lord. He took out all his fears and stared them down, unflinching. Then he set them aside and took refuge in his Lord. And under the stars, he bled.

Trust and courage. More treasures in the dark.

I wish I had found the strength earlier to do what my friend had done. I wish I had chosen to forsake the noise and to hide myself in Christ. He could have whispered to my wounds.

But I was weak, and I squandered way too much time.

Perhaps you have made that mistake too. Maybe you've been sitting for too long on the bench, hurting and afraid.

If so, look up, friend. God is a Redeemer and a Restorer. Just look at George. In the midst of tears and darkness and pain, God slowly mended his ache. God spoke into the wounds, not dismissing them or hiding them, but giving George life beyond them. And even though our painful stories don't always have happy endings, God often chooses to restore in deeply tangible ways. George is now remarried to a fellow missionary—a beautiful nurse from Australia. The two of them are living in Papua New Guinea, starting up a home for children and mothers with AIDS, and they have just adopted their first son. Their faces glow with the light of undying hope.

Yes, Christ restores if we invite him into our pain. I found out later than George did, but better late than never. I didn't find it in the black midnight, but in the daytime hours, in the office of a man named Joshua, my senior pastor, the man who would soon become my boss. Every week, I sat on his couch, and he taught me how to bleed. He asked me intimate, uncomfortable questions about my own heart, and the only way to answer him was to look for myself inside that knot of apathy, sorrow, and fear.

I didn't want to do it. I wanted to go directly to the noble answer. I wanted to stand straight and proclaim that God was good no matter what; that Jack would be okay; that I would be okay, and . . . and . . .

"Those might be the right answers, but you're trying to skip the pain, and it doesn't work that way," Joshua insisted. "There is no shortcut. You have to choose to feel it."

He was right, and every part of me knew it. Thus, I surrendered.

Before those days, I had always scorned the idea of "a good cry" as overly sentimental nonsense. But I was wrong. Honest tears have a positive, healing quality. Grief can be a good thing. And when I turned my grief on, I had trouble turning it off.

I stared down at the carpet and let the tears come. I wept for the drop-off days and for the pickups. I wept for the lack of eye contact and for all the times Jack's words came and went away again. I wept for the guilt of the frustration I harbored with him and for not feeling all the affection I knew I ought to find easily.

I wept for myself, too. I knew I had hurt my family in my numbness. Sara had been patient, but she couldn't wait on me forever. She needed me. My daughters needed me, too, and my sons, and I had kept myself from them.

As I wept, Christ drew nearer. I felt his comfort through Joshua and through my merciful family. I felt Christ's breath in the midnight silence, when all the noise was gone. I was not alone. I would never be alone.

This is what God longs to do for us: He longs to take us by the hand and show us his way through the darkness, past our forgetting places, and over our fears. He leads us to the place of acceptance. Together, friend, we will find a way to face our new normals. And by the blood of the Lamb and the words of our testimonies, we will overcome.[3]

CHAPTER 5

Planting a Garden

IF THERE WAS A MOMENT when a switch flipped inside me, I don't remember it. Like most changes, mine happened the gradual way. Little by little, I emerged from my defenses as I started remembering how to be a father. At some point, I published a blog post on a random site I had just built. I'm pretty sure nobody ever read it, and if they had, they would have forgotten it at once. There was nothing artful or profound in it. I simply said I was ready to get off the bench. I had been a spectator for far too long.

I made at least two important changes at that time. First, I started trying to play with Jack more often. I say "trying" because most of the time, he rebuffed me. Those were gray days; I won't lie. The tiny rejections stung. They probably shouldn't have, but they did. I had to learn to push through them.

Once in a while, though, he would give me these little sideward grins when I was approaching to tickle him. Those were sun spottings amid the clouds. Besides fueling me to push through the soul weariness, those moments did something in Jack, too. I'm sure of it. He became more relaxed. More comfortable with me. Not that it should have surprised me—a boy needs his father. He was finally getting one.

The other change I made was to start educating myself on this thing called autism. I did some formal reading and some informal connecting with other parents online. My wife has always been the insatiable investigator of the family, and up until that time, I had read almost nothing. I had always let her handle it. This is a common trait among depressed special-needs dads, by the way. We are notorious for letting our wives do all the legwork—appointments with doctors and therapists. Autism is an enigma, even for the experts. The sheer amount of conflicting medical information and opinions only serve to reinforce a father's unsettling sense of helplessness.

Perhaps this is why the online autism support community is overwhelmingly female. Moms need to find support somewhere, so many of them turn to Facebook. There they find thousands of other moms and a few dads looking for specific answers, or for a digital shoulder to cry on, or for a group who will listen to an occasional rant about rude family members who tell them, "If you just disciplined your kid, he would be fine."

Of course, while social media can help to meet all those needs, it can also exacerbate your confusion and aggravation. In the same way that Christian platitudes are sandpaper to tortured souls, the autism-themed clichés and inspirational videos circulating on Facebook can make a parent cringe.

One of the first clichés I ran into online went like this: "Autism is like an unplanned trip to Holland." How so, you ask? Well, imagine you were planning an exotic vacation to, say, Venice. Now imagine that when you stepped off the plane, you realized you had arrived in Holland instead. It's a surprise, yes, but Holland is home to some pretty delightful stuff too: windmills and canals and tulips, to name a few. So chin up. Parenting an autistic child won't be what you thought, but you'll still love it!

This must be a helpful sentiment for some people or else it wouldn't be passed around so much, but for a newbie autism dad trying to deal with his son's wordlessness, bowel-control problems, meltdowns, and severe insomnia, this was a maddening message. Holland sounded amazing—and I'd still love to visit there someday, especially given my last name—but at the time it also sounded very, very far away.

Here, my mind was first awakened to the controversial question that draws more heat than any other issue in this community: Is autism a blessing or a curse?

At the time, the answer seemed obvious: Autism had stolen away my son. Of course it wasn't a blessing.

But then came the counterarguments:

Don't you know that autism comes with gifts?

What about the fact that so many savants are on the spectrum?

Einstein would have been put on the spectrum, you know.

Those arguments sounded silly, but they had some merit. Autism often does come with exceptional abilities. But still, those are the exception. Jack wasn't Rain Man. He didn't appear to have any savant-level abilities. And even if he were so smart he could count cards at a casino, how could that ever make up for what autism had taken away? I just wanted to know my son. God created us all for relationship, but Jack couldn't share in this blessing. The "gifts" argument made autism sound exotic, but I found it to be, on the whole, insulting.

There was another argument, however, that gave me pause. It rose up every time someone talked of finding a cure:

"Autism is a blessing because it's a part of a person's identity. It isn't a disease to be cured but a present to be unwrapped."

I knew this was true, at least on some level. Autism is not a disease. You can't find it on an MRI scan or through a blood test. It is invisible, except for the symptoms. Therefore, the logic said, you can't remove it from your child any more than you can remove her sunny disposition.

To look for a cure would be like trying to cure a person's race or gender. Above all, they said, this is a diversity issue. Just as there exists ethnic diversity, there also exists neurodiversity. And like all diversity, we should celebrate it, not mourn it.

I wasn't sure what to make of any of that. Was autism really a part of Jack at such a core level? It would have been helpful to start with a better definition of autism. I didn't really know what it was back then. And even today, all these years later, I'm still not sure I do. I'm not sure anyone does.

Autism spectrum disorder was and is an enigma. Here's how the Mayo Clinic defines it: "A serious neurodevelopmental disorder that impairs a child's ability to communicate and interact with others. It also includes restricted repetitive behaviors, interests and activities. These issues cause significant impairment in social, occupational and other areas of functioning."[1]

This is the first type of thing new autism parents see, which is why so many of us feel crushed and defeated in the early days following a diagnosis. It is a wholly clinical, thoroughly dark, and tragically incomplete description that says nothing of the beauty and richness autistic people bring to this world. It makes no mention of the powerful insights and fascinating perspectives they offer, and it leaves out the stories of their persistent fight to overcome the challenges they face from a world that does not understand them.

Even where such definitions ring true, they almost never ring completely true, because autism is a spectrum. There is a wide variety of symptoms and severity of symptoms depending on the person.

But what lies beneath the symptoms? What is it that causes the "restricted repetitive behaviors" we call "stimming"? What is it that impairs social interaction? Those questions are sources of sharp controversy. Some suggest it's all caused by unalterable genes. Others point to gastro-intestinal problems triggered by environmental factors. Is it nature or is it nurture, or is it some blend of both?

The science is ever evolving, but there is little agreement on any of this. Someday—hopefully soon—it will all be clearer. For now, though, despite all the research, it's very difficult to explain what autism is. We only know what it looks like. And for us, it looks like Jack.

To make matters doubly confusing, autism rarely walks alone. It brings friends, often called "comorbid conditions," meaning conditions that live alongside the autism. For instance, Jack's autism is accented with epilepsy, severe anxiety, and obsessive-compulsive disorder, to name a few. Other people with autism deal with bipolar disorder, ADHD, bowel disease, fragile X syndrome, and a variety of learning disabilities.

The list is long. The spectrum is broad. The knot is tangled and tight. Where does autism end and, say, anxiety begin? It's impossible to say. Truly impossible.

For a father trying to get off the bench, these were troubling revelations that raised even more core questions. How could I face down a future that felt so utterly confounding?

How could I accept something if I didn't understand what it was in the first place?

Even more to the point: *What was I supposed to hope for now?*

Hope. We all long for it when we see it at a distance. We like to see the word in bright-colored fonts spread over inspiring images. Hope is the color of the sun over the grayscale jungles; of seedlets budding on a barren desert floor. Hope as an idea is artful inspiration. But when you hunger and thirst for it as badly as I was, you must be careful. It is not what you think. "Let me tell you something, my friend," Morgan Freeman's character said in *The Shawshank Redemption*. "Hope is a dangerous thing. Hope can drive a man insane."[2]

Since I first began teaching and preaching, hope had been my favorite topic. The first clause of Hebrews 11:1 became my mantra: "Faith is the substance of things hoped for." I felt like everyone was always preaching on faith in the church, but the writer of Hebrews seemed to imply that hope preceded faith. After all, you can't put your belief into action the way faith demands unless you first possess at least some expectation of good.

Were my words wrong? I don't think so. But hope is far more tangible than I thought it was back then. Tangible and volatile. Believing in God's goodness is easy when things are good. But when you are living in the Valley of the Shadow—when you are begging for daily bread in the Land of Unanswered Prayer—it becomes a temptress, seducing us like a desert mirage. The oasis is there for a flash, then it is gone. And even when we really do arrive at cool waters along our journeys, we come with suspicion and doubt, having swallowed too many mouthfuls of sand from our canteens.

I swallowed sand at least two dozen times those first years. We would see something glimmer, and we would get excited. Too excited, as it turned out.

The first time was when we changed Jack's diet. We had just begun our journey at the time and were sucked in by the buzz that the MMR vaccine was the cause of autism. We had no idea that the movement was based on a dubious medical study, nor did we have any context for the controversy that churns around the topic even to this day. All we knew was what we heard: that vaccines were harmful, but that we could reverse the harm by addressing the gastrointestinal issues they triggered.

We read stories of children who had "come back" from autism through changes to their diets alone. Removing the gluten and the dairy, they said, would get us halfway down the road.

So we dutifully pulled out any trace of milk and wheat, and, wonder of wonders, we started to see some improvements. There was a rash on his face that suddenly cleared up, and his behavior evened out significantly.

We rejoiced at his gains. "It's happening," we said, full of new faith. I reached over to my projector and switched it on again. Just for a little while.

But of course, it didn't last. Jack's progress stalled almost right away. We tried a number of variations of vitamins and supplements, but nothing stuck. The rash didn't return as long as we kept him off gluten. The food allergy was real, but there would be no magic-bullet diet.

Fortunately, Jack's early education program—the one behind the silver button—was starting to yield some promising results. His teachers used a method called Applied Behavior Analysis, or ABA, a controversial philosophy (yes, everything is pretty controversial in this realm) that leans heavy on creating routines, offering rewards, and preparing the child for the real world.

This highly intensive, highly structured methodology was beginning to get through to him. Soon he was greeting his teachers and waving good-bye to me at drop-off time. His words became less garbled, and he was starting to learn and deploy new phrases at home: "I want chips, please," for instance. We would hoot and holler and say to ourselves, *He's not that far behind his peers when you think about it.*

The next day, we would try to get him to show these gains to teachers, but he would only offer a blank and silent stare. After school, we would have to teach him the phrase again as if it were the first time. And then the next day. And the next.

I first heard the term *regression* in the early days, and I grew to hate it. We thought Jack's initial regression at two years old would be our new starting point on which to build his future. We were wrong. He would take a giant step forward in his development, then two steps back. He would learn, then unlearn. New regressions kept coming at us like sneaker waves, carrying his victories out to sea and drowning our fresh hopes in the undertow.

Summertime proved most devastating. Routines are essential for kids like Jack, but when school ends, schedules go out the window. We thought he had made lasting strides his first year at the school in Oregon, but he lost them all in July. "Where did Jack go?" his teachers lamented when they saw him again.

Where indeed.

I said before that grief meanders. Hope does too. Some days, the horizon looks close and inviting. Other days, the fog swallows it, and we can't remember what it is we are believing for. No matter the details of our fight, we all have good seasons and bad ones, hours that make hearts glimmer and days that make dreams dull.

How can we move forward under such conditions? How can we ground our feet in sands of hope if the place where we stand feels so unstable?

One thing I knew: I didn't like any of it. If this was what our life was like now—this shell game of promises and setbacks—I didn't want to accept it. I loved my son, and I knew he was a blessing, but in my weakened state, I could not puzzle out how this particular blend of symptoms could possibly be something worth celebrating.

This is a shared dilemma in the Land of Unanswered Prayer, and one of our chief concerns as followers of Christ:

How then shall we walk? How should we carry ourselves in the midst of our trials? Is it okay to walk with a slumped back, or should we straighten up and start to whistle? To say it even more bluntly: Do we have to celebrate what we're going through in order to embrace it in a healthy, godly way?

For this question, I turn to one of the most painful events in all of Scripture: the destruction of Jerusalem in 586 BC. This would have been a painful event for any people, but for the children of Israel, it was a crushing blow.

They were the chosen people. God had promised them the stars. He would turn them into a great kingdom, and a descendant of David would sit on the throne forever. God had vowed to bless them, to protect them, and to make them a shining example of perfect goodness and enduring strength.

Now, hundreds of years after those initial promises, the covenant was in ashes. They had broken it again and again and again. For many decades, God tried to warn them of the terrible consequences of their idolatry. He sent prophet after prophet to warn them of their impending doom. They could turn back. There was still time.

Jeremiah's calls were especially moving. The Babylonians were rising, he said, and unless Judah repented of her idolatry, they would swallow Jerusalem whole.

But the people preferred their old propaganda films to such warnings. Destruction could happen to others, but not to them. They were God's chosen people.

Even when the mighty Nebuchadnezzar at last laid siege to Jerusalem, many still couldn't believe they would lose the fight. But soon food ran out, the wells went dry, the walls were breached, and the city burned.

Thousands died, either from starvation or the sword. Those who survived watched the soldiers utterly destroy their beloved Temple—the symbol of their covenant-keeping God. It was a bitter day.

Their misery didn't end there, however. Thousands of survivors were forced to leave their decimated homeland. They marched under armed guard for almost nine hundred miles.[3] It would have taken weeks. Months, even. They passed through many regions on that walk. They would have passed through the now-defunct northern kingdom, through the outskirts of Syria, and through the Euphrates River valley. And unless I'm wrong, they also walked through the initial stages of grief as well: denial, anger, bargaining.

After their arrival in ancient Babylon, they were neck deep in sadness. Psalm 137 paints the scene, giving off the unmistakable scent of depression:

By the waters of Babylon,
    there we sat down and wept,
    when we remembered Zion.
On the willows there
    we hung up our lyres.
For there our captors

required of us songs,
and our tormentors, mirth, saying,
  "Sing us one of the songs of Zion!"

How shall we sing the LORD's song
  in a foreign land?

PSALM 137:1-4, ESV

Their heritage was gone, and everywhere they looked, the survivors saw reminders of their own humiliation: emblems of great riches, pagan gods, and overwhelming military might.

Apparently there were other prophets trying to encourage them with foretellings of a quick liberation.[4] God would take vengeance on Babylon, they insisted, and the exiles would be back home in no time. Their defeat was really just a small and temporary setback. Soon a new army would rise up, a new Temple would be built, and who knows, there might even be a new shepherd boy waiting to become king!

Those perpetually optimistic voices still reach us in the present. "This thing you're going through is but a hiccup," people say. Their hearts are pure. They only want to encourage us. "None of it will last. You're about to be done!"

Such guarantees were not helpful in ancient Israel, and they aren't very helpful now. Optimists, God love them, are no more able to tell the future than pessimists are. Don't get me wrong; we need hopeful voices in our lives. But some circumstances are past the point of easy fixing. Sometimes a disease is terminal; sometimes a marriage is broken beyond repair; sometimes the exile lasts. In such cases, unbridled optimism has no power to deliver on its promises.

What then? Is the only alternative to give in to permanent despair? Certainly it can't all be sorrow. Is there nothing to be thankful for in the present fight? Are there no roses in the midst of all the thorns? Is there no cool breeze on the banks of the Euphrates? Every time we inhale, we breathe in God's continued blessing. We have life. We have breath. We have this day. He has not forgotten us.

This is the same tug-of-war that rages in the special-needs community. Parents like me can feel so awash in sorrow that they can no longer see the beauty of their children, while advocates on the spectrum are begging the world to look past the pain and see the loveliness autism can offer.

So now, we join the exiles on the banks of the river as we stand between two different visions of life. How shall we live in our Land of Unanswered Prayer? How can we embrace our long exile?

The prophet Jeremiah himself gave the Israelites their answer in a letter sent to the first wave of exiles. We've all heard the most memorable line of that letter. It goes like this:

"I know the plans that I have for you," declares the LORD, "plans for welfare and not for calamity to give you a future and a hope."

JEREMIAH 29:11, NASB

How ironic that we have plastered that line on the front of graduation cards and fancy memes about hope, when in fact, it came directly after this sobering sentence:

> For thus says the LORD, "When seventy years have been completed for Babylon, I will visit you and fulfill My good word to you, to bring you back to this place."
>
> JEREMIAH 29:10, NASB

Put together, those lines promise something along these lines: "God hasn't forgotten Israel, and he still has plans to bring your people back home—plans that he will accomplish after most of you are long dead."

You can almost see the slumping shoulders of the exiles as they read that they would not be rescued. In this case, there would be no cure for what ailed them. There would be no escape from Babylon, no matter what the prognosticators claimed.

The rest of the letter gives keen instructions on how to live out the remainder of their lives. Jeremiah's tone is at once subdued and sanguine:

> Thus says the LORD of hosts, the God of Israel, to all the exiles whom I have sent into exile from Jerusalem to Babylon, "Build houses and live in them; and plant gardens and eat their produce. Take wives and become the fathers of sons and daughters, and

take wives for your sons and give your daughters to
husbands, that they may bear sons and daughters;
and multiply there and do not decrease. Seek the
welfare of the city where I have sent you into exile,
and pray to the LORD on its behalf; for in its welfare
you will have welfare."

JEREMIAH 29:4-7, NASB

Yes, I know he wrote these words for his lonely countrymen,
but they are mine now. They are yours, too. And today, the
prophet is urging both of us to make peace with our situations. It is true that we must come to a place of acceptance,
but acceptance will probably be bittersweet. Indeed, the
bitter flavors might be the most potent. After all, Babylon
might be pretty this time of year, but it is not home. It is
not Jerusalem. Thankfully, there is no law requiring us to
feel affection for a thing before we embrace it.

But please hear me: We need to embrace it.

What does this mean for me? It means I have to make
peace with my son's condition every day. I don't have to
pretend I am enjoying it on days when I am not, but neither can I ignore the beauty and blessings it offers on the
other days. I don't have to commit to any polarizing camp.

If Jack's regressions continue for the rest of his life, I
will have to make the best of it. I will have to open my eyes
wide to discover who he is instead of who he is not, and the
truest thing about him is that he is precious. Every one of
his thirty-seven trillion cells carries the fingerprints of his

Creator. Joy sits in his eyes, and it is my job to find that joy and to fan it wherever it flickers; to take his hand whenever he falters; to give him the words he so desperately wants. My job is to find the gold within him, even when he himself doesn't see it, and help him mine it out.

This is my life in exile, and I realized it sometime in the middle of that season of regressions. I'm not sure when the lesson took, but it took, and I finally waved good-bye to sorrow.

What about for you, friend? I don't know your trials, but I know this: They might always hurt. The feeling of misplaced pain might never go away. You cannot beat yourself up over that. The trial you're dealing with might never inspire happiness, but that cannot be your end game. If it is, you are setting yourself up for a lifetime of guilt and self-loathing.

And yet there will be joy in this journey. I promise you, there will be aching joy. It is the greatest of all the treasures of the dark. We'll find it together.

For now, let's settle in. God plays the long game. We are playing it now too. The days of despairing and self-medicating have to end. It's time to plant a garden.

CHAPTER 6

It's Not All Rubble

HERE IS WHERE WE ARE so far on this journey: The first step to embracing aching joy is to embrace the aching. I'm not a psychologist, and I don't pretend to understand all the ways people mend, but this was how I mended. Before I could learn joy, I had to move toward the places of pain one by one: the denial and churning anger, the bargaining and dark depression, and finally the bittersweet acceptance of life's new terms.

My biggest struggle throughout this process was one of hope management. I had tried to shut off my expectations early on—that stubborn, sputtering projector in my mind. Expectations can soar and crash in a single afternoon.

This is one of the reasons grief meanders as it does, and one of the reasons acceptance is so difficult to attain: Our hope is always recalibrating. In my world, a new string of well-deployed vocabulary words can make Jack's future suddenly appear bright, but a meltdown on the sidewalk can make me think we'll never see the sun again. Those emotional reactions are natural, I suppose, but as my friend Nathan in California once told me, "We have to be careful we do not learn too much from any one situation."

I made that mistake one afternoon when Jack was still in his early-intervention program. It happened so quickly and so subtly that I didn't even realize I had done it, but the repercussions were far-reaching.

It was a sunny afternoon, which is rare in Oregon. I was picking up Jack from his school behind the silver button. He had just suffered a massive regression. It might have been because of spring break the week before, but I can't be sure. We had been talking with his doctors about it, and his teachers were putting their heads together too. Regressions are common with autistic children, but not like this. This wasn't normal, and everyone could feel it.

There had been speculation about seizures and even strokes, so we ran a battery of tests to try to get a reading on it, but Jack doesn't do well with tests. My poor wife sat with him through an entire sleep study, and they both barely came out of it in one piece. Tests are costly for my boy. They make him extraordinarily anxious. He had flailed and thrashed his way through those examinations, so when the results came back negative, the doctors didn't much trust their own findings.

We were left with nothing, then. No evidence of seizures or strokes; just mystery setbacks. It was maddening.

Without any evidence of comorbid conditions that
might be taking away his gains, Jack's teachers and therapists took their own stab at what might be going on. They
weren't general-education teachers, but rather autism
experts who had been meticulous in their documentation.
They had ridden Jack's ups and downs right alongside us,
and on this afternoon, they gave us their findings.

The hallway was dim, and I was about to slide open the
jail bars and collect my son when his teacher called me to
step aside. She lowered her voice.

"Jason, we don't know what's causing his regressions,"
she said at last, "but we think he might be retarded."

At that, my stomach clenched, and I could feel my head
go light.

I kept a good face on, I think. I thanked her and nod-
ded and took Jack by the hand. No, it was okay, I assured
her. I understood, and we suspected this, and thank you so
much for the honesty.

The word *retarded* has slipped out of favor in recent
years, and the word *retard* even more so. It's easy to understand why. The word has long been used as a cruel epithet,
a schoolyard taunt. The "r-word" is now scorned above all
others in special-needs circles. It is a low thing to mock a
person by comparing him to the most vulnerable members
of a society.

Before it was an insult, however, the r-word held

practical significance, simply referring to a person suffering mental retardation. A retarded person was someone who could not learn or grow anymore. Their progress was hindered. Stopped. Retarded.

Jack's teacher was a kindhearted woman who had always adored my son. I knew what she meant, and yet her words stung all the more because of it. She wasn't mocking him; she only meant he might have an intellectual disability that was retarding his growth. Stopping it.

In other words, he couldn't make progress, so I might as well shut down hope for good. She didn't say that, of course, but in my weakened state, that's what I heard, and that's what I did.

Prior to that conversation, I had learned how to regulate my propaganda machine. I had stopped watching my old daydreams of what my life with Jack would be like, and I would only turn it back on in my weaker, starry-eyed moments.

The waves of progress and regress had taken their toll, though. I had already started to fear that Jack would never be able to retain any forward motion. I worried we might just be seasick forevermore, that every gain would be turned to loss and every celebration would go hollow.

That concern finally crystalized at the words *We think he might be retarded*. When I heard them, I made an unconscious decision not just to turn off my expectations but also to beat them senseless. I destroyed my projector until all the clicking and humming stopped and the bulb was shattered. It only took about ten seconds. By the time we reached the silver button at the exit, the deed was done.

I don't know how I drove home that day, so heavy was my crying. It was my worst day.

The next few months were a slog. Sara rejected the teacher's words outright, but I couldn't shake them.

Fortunately, I wasn't alone in any of it. My church's pastoral staff helped me process it all. By that time, I had joined them on the church-leadership team. It had all happened quite by accident. After I had sat and emptied my soul on Pastor Joshua's couch for a solid year, he took me out to lunch and offered me a job. The church needed an associate pastor, he said. Someone who was a good teacher and could help shoulder the sermon load while overseeing various areas of discipleship. I had already filled the pulpit for him four times that year, and my teaching experience made me a natural fit for the job.

Still, I confess I was baffled by the offer. I reminded him that I was walking through my dark night of the soul. I was at my lowest point and had nothing left to give. In fact, I said that to the entire elder board right before they unanimously voted to bring me on. Nobody seemed to mind the fact that I was weak and depressed. They knew what they were getting into and had committed to carry me through my season of depression, however long it took.

"We won't let you fail," they told me.

They had already made good on that commitment too. Even before the job offer, the entire church had surrounded our family and celebrated my son. Now they were pledging to surround me as I took on official church responsibilities. They shielded me from stresses of the job that could have overwhelmed me in my pitiful state, and they made ample space for me to process and heal. It was a generous arrangement.

Besides that, they also showed great interest in helping the special-needs community. As the staff realized how difficult it was for our family to come to church with a boy who couldn't hang with the standard church classes for kids, they proceeded to help us develop a separate classroom specifically for special-needs children. That way, families like us who craved community support, spiritual encouragement, and a peaceful morning at church could actually find those things.

We knew there was no volunteer capable of running this sort of classroom with the variety of needs and challenges these kids had. We needed an expert, so the church hired Lori, a wonderful and talented woman who had been one of Jack's teachers in his early-intervention days. She loved our boy, and he loved her, too, and that was the beginning of the Open Heavens Room. Over the years, it has become a beautiful and significant aspect of our church's ministry, but it started as a simple gesture from people who cared enough to ask us what we needed—namely Joshua, our pastor, and Janell, our administrator. I could not have asked or prayed for more generous, caring friends than these.

Another aspect of their generosity, it turned out, was

their willingness to listen to my ramblings. I had just discovered that writing could be healing for me, and Joshua
indulged me by listening to my half-baked story ideas and
blog posts.

One afternoon, I sat on the couch in his office and
read aloud a lousy short story I had just written. A whole
year had passed since my worst day at Jack's school, and
I had mostly entered into the season of acceptance. If my
story had been better, I might have just inserted it into this
chapter, but it wasn't good. It was too self-serious, and the
metaphors didn't work. Nevertheless, the broad strokes of
the story reveal much about how the words *We think he
might be retarded* had shaped my heart, so I'll tell you how
it went:

We open with a father named Philip pulling his car
up to a dilapidated graveyard. His wife is in the car,
and his seven-year-old autistic son is too. The boy
starts melting down, but his wife urges Philip out of
the car and on to his mission.

So he gets out of his car and takes his backpack
with him. The cemetery is full of dead soldiers whose
monuments have been taken over by weeds. He
walks past all of them and arrives at an empty grave,
a hole in the ground that he himself had dug the day
before.

Here, Philip kneels down and opens his
backpack. He takes out a baseball bat and traces the

grains of wood with his fingers. He closes his eyes and replays a vision of a young ballplayer knocking a low pitch deep into left field. The crowd goes crazy.

Philip opens his eyes, exhales, and puts the bat into the empty grave.

Next, he pulls out a picture of a young bride and groom and clutches it to his chest. He closes his eyes again and begins to cry. In his mind's eye, he sees that handsome young man in a tuxedo feigning nervousness at the front of the church. He's posing up there, hamming it up. Then, the groom sees her step into the aisle, and his knees go limp.

The father wipes his eyes, then opens them, laying the wedding picture in the hole next to the bat.

There are other items too: A diploma. Sunglasses. A pocketknife. A copy of Plato's *Republic*. All of them he lays to rest. All of them he weeps over. They are remnants of a life lost; they are rubble.

But just before he shovels the dirt onto them, he sees something that doesn't belong: There is a price tag on the bat. He reaches down and peels it off. In fact, there are price tags on all the items.

And here, the audience is supposed to realize the shift: This father is not seeing his past, but his lost future. He is not mourning the death of a grown son, but rather the lost future of the son he now has: the autistic son who was melting down in the car. These aren't old family treasures; they are stand-in items he had just picked up from the store for this occasion. Even the picture is just a frame with a placeholder image. Philip is burying his hopes. Or, for our purposes, we might say he is destroying his projector.

When the deed is done, he returns to his wife and son a free man, no longer a slave to his dreams that would never be realized. They would make a new future now, the three of them.

As I said, the story didn't work, but I was fairly proud of it at the time and had expected Joshua to share in my enthusiasm. He is a naturally exuberant fellow and gives out "attaboys" liberally. This time, though, he sat still and wore a grimace.

"You don't like it?" I asked.

He shifted in his chair. "No, it's good, it's just . . . it's not rubble," he said.

I shook my head, not understanding.

He tried again. "The stuff he buried. It's not rubble. It's not junk."

I smiled. He didn't understand. How could he? "Yeah, it was junk. It was just stuff in his own mind."

"I get that, but that stuff has value, too. It's better than rubble."

We discussed it for a few minutes, but I didn't budge. It was rubble. Nobody knew that as well as I did. I've always respected Joshua's wisdom, but he wasn't a special-needs dad, so I couldn't expect him to understand that Philip's actions were heroic. But they were—I knew it firsthand, for I, too, had buried my dreams for my son.

And maybe it was a noble decision, in some small way. I only wanted to prove that I loved Jack unconditionally, that I could accept and embrace him even if he never made any progress, even if we never shared an inside joke or threw a football in the yard. I only wanted to silence the projector that had made false promises.

Little did I realize I had merely traded in one set of ordered expectations for another. While destroying that propaganda machine in my head, I had inadvertently set up a new one. Rather than playing all the sappy family fantasies, this one played all the safe, sad melodramas and promised to never again raise my expectations—because hope deferred doesn't just make the heart sick; it makes it scared.

This is why I put myself in the story, cursing away my desires as mere rubble—lifeless and colorless, but with sharp, pointy edges, never to be examined again. I was exhausted from disappointment.

These new propaganda films expected and required nothing at all from my son. He was who he was, and that was that. Our life together would be defined by distance. He would struggle mightily, and we would struggle too. He would not grow, but we would love him still, on and on for the rest of our grayscale lives.

This is the picture I had come to accept. This is the soil

in which I was planting a garden. It was a sad place, but at least there would be no more grim surprises. There was safety, I believed, in pessimism.

We pessimists rarely own up to what we are. We call ourselves "realists," as if our dark outlook were any closer to reality than that of those poor saps who think something good might happen in this world. If the church is full of optimistic, happy-go-lucky faces insisting everything is fine, our larger Western world stands at the opposite end: a dramatic culture enamored by romantic tragedy. Only the suffering know what real life is. If they live happy lives, they do so only because they are privileged.

Real life, in the eyes of our Western sophists, is pain. We suffer and cry, and then we die. We make movies about said suffering, and the critics rave. Think about it: How many comedies ever receive an Academy Award nomination? Is that even allowed? Nearly all the most acclaimed books and films are those which celebrate sadness, dying, and heroic tragedy.

The Land of Unanswered Prayer is full of people like me—people who have lost their optimism. People who spend sleepless nights waiting for another shoe to drop. Many of us then seek to protect ourselves by lowering our expectations to minimal levels. We trade hope for safety.

Hear me, friend: This is not a sound exchange.

I know, I know—I keep telling you to embrace the pain in whatever form it comes. I keep telling you to eschew fantasy and meet your aching straight on. All this is true.

But it will do you no good to hurl yourself in the other direction either.

Aching is a part of our existence, and it always will be. But then, so is joy. There will be storms, but there will also be days with gentle breezes, blue skies, and seventy-five-degree temperatures. Is one day any more solid than the other? Is a pessimist's world any more realistic than the optimist's? Neither has much control over the world, but both will taste hardships as well as blessings.

I made a grievous miscalculation when I let my hope die the way I did. In doing so, I became an enemy of surprise. I put a cap on what God could do, on what my son could do, and on how much I could grow.

This is why we must be wary of which voices we pay allegiance to. In the world of autism, for instance, we hear many voices. The prognostications of doctors and specialists can be devastating. They sometimes say things like "Your son will probably never learn to speak," or "Your little girl is not capable of empathy," or "Don't expect her to ever make friends."

I'm not suggesting we ignore these pronouncements. We should listen to and ponder them. But why should we swallow them whole? Do you know how many children have been sentenced to these futures and yet have overcome them?

But this isn't about autism; it's about you. You will hear the pronouncements, too, if you haven't already. Your situation is full of questions and uncertainties, and voices will emerge to fill those uncertainties. They will tell you that nothing will ever improve. They will tell you to shut the door to the possibility that anything will change or that your heart will ever heal. They will tell you to go into the hope-management system and lower the bar until it's level with your ankles. They might even know what they're talking about.

It might look hopeless from where you sit. Indeed, it makes no sense to keep hoping for good things if we are on our own, or if God is dead. But what if he lives? What if the songs we sing on Sundays are true? What if God's Spirit is yet active in this world? How could we ever surrender completely to sorrow? How could we shut the door to the intervening hand of a saving God?

You are hurting, I know, and you have a right to your pain. Jesus Christ, too, was a Man of Sorrows, a man who wept.[1] You are a child of the Most High King, and as such, you have privileges:

You have permission to admit the truth when you are hurting.

You have permission to feel fear at grief's dark hours.

You have permission to ask, "Why have you forsaken me?"

You have permission to weep for hours on end.

You even have permission to embrace a thing without celebrating it.

But as a child of God and a follower of Jesus, you are forbidden one thing: You are not allowed to give up hope.

I understand the tension. What I'm asking of you is not

easy: to let go and to keep holding on at the same time; to surrender your deepest longings while trusting that an invisible God might breathe some life into them still. But hope is not yours to kill. It never was. Hope is a gift for you to hold, not to control. You hold only the end of a vine stretching heavenward, and you must tend it, even in the winter months. You must keep it alive.

These are hard things. It would be far easier to smother the cries of our hearts. There would be less pain that way. But the moment we cut ourselves off from the possibility of sorrow, we also cut ourselves off from laughter. We cannot numb only one side of our hearts.

There is a way forward on this journey, and it is narrow. It requires that we refuse protective measures and remain vulnerable. We must keep our hearts open to disappointment and surprise. We must continue to risk heartbreak.

If there were only weeping, I would have despaired. I would have allowed my new, safe fantasies to play on forever. Fortunately, I discovered that my culture was wrong. Joy could be every bit as tangible as aching. And I was finally about to find it.

PART 2

Finding Joy

 es

CHAPTER 7

The In-Between Country

IN A WORLD AS DAMAGED AS OURS, sorrow comes easily, but I have never been able to manufacture joy. We Christians often talk about "choosing joy," but it isn't a sweater we can pull from an internal wardrobe of emotions. It isn't one of those virtues we can attain by seeking it. Oh, we can try to drum it up and force it onto our faces, but when we do, we head right back into denial. "Yes, ma'am. Everything's fine, ma'am. We're all just fine. Thank you, ma'am, for asking."

Joy doesn't produce itself either. It is a by-product. This is why Paul categorized it as a fruit of the Spirit—a prize of a greater Branch. It grows from relationships, mind-sets, or situations. When we see where we are—that is, when we come to grips with our circumstances—we have a choice:

We can reject the gladness budding from those limbs, or we can arise, pick, and eat.

In my experience, joy grew slowly—almost imperceptibly. There was no sudden miracle that took away my pain, no rainbow that spilled on my roof. Rather, there were a series of ideas and suggestions that I began to see growing, little by little, until I could no longer ignore them or argue them away. Those ideas elbowed their way into my aching circle. If I was going to remain perpetually sad, I could only do so by denying what was set before me. In the end, joy became a disruption to my sorrow. Joy did not negate my aching, but it broke its monopoly.

The disruption began years earlier, I think, when we saw a video of a severely autistic teenage girl named Carly.[1] Against all odds, Carly learned to communicate by typing. She was nonverbal, so her parents were stunned at her sudden ability to express herself. She later explained that she could understand everything people said and that she wanted to interact with the world around her. It was her body, not her mind, that refused to cooperate. Beneath her disability, Carly was an intelligent, creative, and thoughtful young woman.

The video stuck with us. Why? It wasn't because we thought Jack might learn to communicate like that. Carly's story was clearly an outlier. No, it was the possibility that deep down, below the stifling fog of autism, Jack might be more awake than we ever suspected. He might be listening and understanding us. He might have real, rational reasons for doing what he did. In short, we were intrigued by the possibility of *more*.

It's easy to look at children with severe special needs and assume they are on autopilot. We look at the little girl squealing and laughing at the clouds, or the boy with the funny helmet spinning round and round in the grocery store, and we conclude, "That's just what they do."

Carly's story gave us a different paradigm: Always assume competence. Nonverbal doesn't mean nonthinking.

Take flapping, for instance. Ever since he was three years old, Jack has been a flapper. If you were to see him wandering around town or through the living room, he would probably be carrying two bendable items with which to flap at hummingbird speed. His instruments don't have to be identical, but they have to be similar. Socks work well, as do lanyards and laminated pages.

We thought Jack's flapping was an automatic tick at first, but as we learned about the sensory nature of autism, that changed. If Jack is anything like the self-advocates who describe their own experiences (and he probably is), flapping is a way of calming the madness around him. Our world is altogether too bright, too loud, and too unpredictable for those with high sensitivity to external stimuli. It would be like my having to live inside a Chuck E. Cheese's. The blinking lights . . . the incessant screaming . . . the unmistakable stench of sweaty cheese . . . It's enough to make me want to hide inside a rat costume. (But I digress.)

Flapping seems to help calm Jack's world by giving him something predictable. You should see him. When he flaps, he leans in and squints through his whirling instruments toward a picture, or a favorite toy, or even a family member. Whatever he sees inside that effect, it captivates him, and he can't get enough of it. Flapping is the one thing he can control. One thing he can count on.

That might seem like a small, inconsequential theory, but the implications were interesting. If Jack had his own rationale for flapping, he might have reasons for doing other things too.

Take wandering, for instance. Jack has been a flight risk for most of his life. His insatiable desire to get out and run gave us cold sweats for years. One day, he disappeared and returned before we ever realized what had happened. We saw him running around inside the house with two shiny silver coasters, and we wondered where they had come from. But we just shrugged. He was enjoying turning them upside down to let the light bounce around the room. We let it go.

Then we heard a knock at our front door. Our next-door neighbor was standing there, red faced and roaring with laughter. She told us she had just come home to find that her silver coasters were missing from her living room—and in their place sat two pairs of little-boy underwear. She knew our son well. He had not only found a way out without us knowing but had also gone on a successful mission. He had made an exchange.

Jack's wandering and flapping were evidence that he possessed the same sort of preferences and opinions that every kid possesses, and his coaster exchange indicated a boyish intentionality—a sense of humor, even. All of it pointed to comprehension. All of it whispered, "There is more to your boy than you can imagine. It is there, buried beneath the fog."

You would think those whispers would have brought us some relief or excitement, but they didn't. Not really. In some ways, it meant his situation was sadder than we had once thought. If wandering and flapping hinted at a much deeper well of comprehension, then our boy might be living in constant frustration with his own limbs and his own tongue. It meant he might have his own real desires and dreams, most of which, barring some seismic shift, would stay locked inside him his whole life.

So we moved forward, all of us, and learned to make the best of the challenges we knew might never go away. We talked to Jack as if he would understand every word. No baby talk. If he had a speech therapy appointment, we would tell him ahead of time. We would try to get a picture of the therapist to show him. No need to add surprise to anxiety. We would carry out one-sided conversations with him, asking him questions, and offering leading answers. We taught our daughters, Emily and Jenna, to do the same: Always presume competence.

I wonder, though, whether Jack could hear the differences in the ways we spoke to him. Whereas Sara's tone was warm and open, mine, I fear, was stale and condescending. When she would pause after she asked him a question, it seemed she actually expected a response, despite the overwhelming odds. I don't think I sounded like that. No, I *know* I didn't. And there was no excuse either. When I make up Cowboy Pete stories for my kids, or when I stand on stage and preach about Elijah the prophet, my voice has color in it. When I sit in my living room and rant about how terrible the Star Wars prequels were, I get worked up. I know how to engage in communication.

With Jack, however, there was no engagement. There was only resignation. In my mind, Jack and I were both stuck. Not only would I never see the fulfillment of my own backyard dreams for my son, but his own dreams, whatever they were, would also surely remain out of reach, stuck in stasis forever.

This was what grew from the pieces of hope I had buried in the graveyard. This was the shade of my new posture. If depression was bathed in grays, acceptance sat soaking in sepia. I wasn't sad, but I wasn't happy either. My emotions were content right where they were, in all their muted glory. In hindsight, it was a predictable result. Good fruit cannot grow from rubble, after all.

I carried that mind-set on my shoulder and dutifully began to plant my garden by the rivers of Babylon. And that was when the English preacher shook me out of my funk with his fateful invitation: "If you are the parent of a special-needs child, I'd like you to come up and get prayer."

If he had asked that a few months before, I might have been eager to obey. But I was sure I didn't need prayer anymore. I had settled down. Those poor saps with unrealistic expectations—they were the ones who needed prayer. But I was past that. I had evolved. I had purged myself of fantasy.

I don't remember anything that safe Canadian ministry student said, except one word: *breakthrough*. That word knocked me to the floor amid a rush of blinding tears. In the span of four and a half seconds, I lost all my gains. I was back where I began, staring blurry-eyed at a broken projector screen.

It was the Canadian's fault, of course. People of his ilk take Jesus' instructions literally. They pray God's Kingdom would move from heaven to earth. It is an audacious prayer, for it reminds us all that wholeness actually exists. There really is a place where health is the norm, and there really is an appointed day when our world will experience full restoration. "A new heaven and a new earth," John promised (Revelation 21:1). And when it arrives, Christ will be sitting on his throne, in full command of every bit of brokenness that sunk the hearts of men. And the fight will, at last, be over.

> He will wipe away every tear from their eyes, and death shall be no more, neither shall there be mourning, nor crying, nor pain anymore, for the former things have passed away.
>
> REVELATION 21:4, ESV

I feel the truth of that promise. My own longing bears witness to the reality of that world and the coming of that day. For as C. S. Lewis said, we only possess desires for things that actually exist: food and water, sleep and sex—and "if I find in myself a desire which no experience in this world can satisfy, the most probable explanation is that I was made for another world."[2]

What in this realm can satisfy our universal thirst for health and wholeness? We simply cannot find it. Not amid volcanoes and cancers, blizzards and bereavements, cold-blooded cruelty and violent indifference. Here, we find rejection that leads to addiction, and shame that leads to suicide. Here, we find a hundred million hungry orphans who have never tasted trust. Our world is a war zone of wills, a whirlwind of sickness, a collision of selfish lusts. We find many things here, but perfect wholeness is not among them.

And yet the longing persists, no matter how hard we try to smother it. I felt it again that night at the mere mention of breakthrough, and it brought me to my knees. You've felt it too. The longing throbs when you pass the graveyard, and it blares under the flashing lights of the ambulance. You've even felt it in the regret that comes after a moment of swift selfishness.

"It's not supposed to be this way," it says. "It was never supposed to be this way. Sickness is a trespasser. Sin and death are shadowy brigands we were never supposed to meet. The harsh symptoms of severe autism were never invited here."

Truly, we were made for another world where those invaders cannot go. And one day, the boundaries of that beautiful country will extend even to the Land of Unanswered Prayer. On that day, the stubborn promise burning in our bones will finally be fulfilled. Not just my desires, but my son's, too. My Jack will be free from all his comorbid captors. No longer will he squeal and rage against his uncooperative limbs. No longer will panic seize him and toss him to the floor. His tongue will be unfrozen and his heart set free. Every sentiment he's ever wanted to share can finally come pouring out.

Breakthrough. It's all I've ever wanted. The Canadian's prayer pushed me out of space and time. I didn't want to wait until Restoration Day to hear Jack's songs; I wanted to hear them right then—that night. I was weary of waiting. I am still weary of waiting.

For now, Jack and I stand where you stand. We wait in God's Kingdom, which is at once *already* and *not yet*. Christ came to us once, dying and rising to inaugurate his rule. When he ascended, he invited us to join in his campaign of comforting the afflicted, healing the sick, and praying God's will be done. It is not done yet, but it will be.

We walk toward that day as ambassadors not only of Christ but also of his unfinished Kingdom. As followers of Jesus, we wear the badge of promise on our chests as the insignia of our true home and the promise of breakthrough.

When my Canadian friend stood and prayed that night, he knew well the promise of Restoration Day. He also knew the odds of getting a miracle on that evening. Miracles rarely happen in this age. And still, he asked. This is not only the mark of an ambassador but also the mark of a son. This is what Christ calls us to do.

Breakthrough didn't come that night for Jack. I didn't get my miracle. But the mere request reminded me that breakthrough was not fiction. That prayer snapped my mind back to a truth I had long neglected: Jack's struggle will one day end. And on that day, he will receive a double honor.

> People will come from east and west, and from north
> and south, and recline at table in the kingdom of
> God. And behold, some are last who will be first,
> and some are first who will be last.
>
> LUKE 13:29-30, ESV

Who does this apply to if not those with severe disabilities? Throughout history, they have been overlooked, abused, and derided. It would be bad enough if it were just their own bodies that hurt them, but the culture does too. In every generation, they have lived life in the back of the line. They have been "last." But on Restoration Day, the honor will be reversed.

I try to imagine the scene: my Jack at the head of the banquet table, in full command of his faculties. He is telling jokes up there. Everyone's laughing. His face is full of delight. And he has friends there too. Real friends. I

imagine him calling the name of a boy three chairs down.
They pound their fists together and begin to relive their
adventures. I see him lean over to kiss his mother on the
cheek and pin a flower on her blouse. It's blue, his favorite
color. I see him raise up a song from a Disney movie, and
everyone joins in. When it ends, he begins to tease his siblings about the quality of their singing. He is merciless, but
none of them can stop laughing.

And then he turns to me, gripping my shoulder. We
lock eyes. They stay locked. He can see the tears welling
up in mine, so he smiles, and he reminds me of a time he
had been upset but couldn't tell me why. At last, he can
explain what was wrong. And I try to listen because I want
to know—I really do—but all I can manage is to think to
myself, *My son was lost, but now he is found.*

G. K. Chesterton once called joy "the gigantic secret
of the Christian."[3] I don't think he meant that Christians
are the only ones who can experience it. Rather, he meant
that Christians have an evergreen claim to it. As long as we
clutch the hand of Christ, we hold the hope of Restoration
Day. It is not always an obvious hope. It might well be a
quiet, barely glowing ember lying amid the dust of doubt
and circumstance. But still, even in that hidden, secret
state, it is grounds enough for joy.

I won't try to tell you it's enough to beat back the aching.
It wasn't for me. Not at first. Just as grief meanders and hope
wanes, joy is a fire that needs tending. The hope of heaven
might not keep you going. On any given day, it might be too

cloudy. Too ethereal. Too distant. But patience, friend. This is only the first taste. There will be more.

I couldn't see this vision in the beginning. Talk of eternity can confuse and bruise those who are in the midst of fresh grief. We have to begin by simply following Jesus through this Land of Unanswered Prayer. Jesus embraced his pain. He chose to feel all of it and give it all to God. I had to do the same. I had to surrender.

But when I did, he beckoned my heart forward to a hill and called me to look up. When I did, I saw this place in a new light. It wasn't just the Land of Unanswered Prayer I was living in—it was the in-between country, a borderland between desolation and restoration, between the two comings of Jesus.

Friend, if your faith is in Christ, I implore you: Look up and see this place in the light of heaven's glow. Sorrow might lurk behind us, yes, but before us sits a celestial city on a hill, the promise of full redemption.

Our time here is valuable. Our life has supreme worth. But our existence in this land is short. Soon, Christ will come again with heaven's armies. Justice will ride on his shoulder. He will hold a bow of healing, with a quiver full of peace. And before him, all the demigods will bend their knee—every deceit of the heart, every disease of the body, and every disorder of the mind. All of us, together, will be made new.

For now, we wait in the in-between country.

CHAPTER 8

The Penguin Incident

"HONESTLY, I JUST THINK sometimes you're in a little bit of denial."

I was sitting with Sara in a booth at a Portland pizzeria, and we were finally having the discussion we had almost had a dozen times before. I had always been afraid to voice my concerns about denial, but the smell of perfect pepperoni must have relaxed my inhibitions.

She just smiled at me. A patient smile. I don't think I had offended her, but that comment came close. I pressed on.

"It's just that sometimes you say you think he's made all this progress, but I don't see it at all. I think sometimes you see what you want to see."

She took a bite of her salad. (Actually, I have no idea what she was eating that night. She's gluten free, though, and she loves her salad like Jack loves flappers, so I think it is a safe imaginary detail.)

"No, I don't think that's true," she said in a calm tone.

But I had given this a lot of thought, and I wouldn't budge. I knew all about denial and lingering expectations. I was kind of an expert, if you don't mind my saying so. This should have been a teachable moment—for her.

She wouldn't budge either, though. She just did that thing where she nods and gives this half smile that says—in the sweetest, stubbornest way possible—"Nope."

Then she went on to sweetly and stubbornly suggest that perhaps I just wasn't watching closely enough. Maybe I needed to be more observant. But see, that was a cheap shot, because both of us know that I never notice anything.

The debate ended with shrugs and smiles, and life went on. Our family was doing pretty well by then. I had become a present father again, having regained some of my lost joy.

Jack was seven years old and attending our local elementary school. I would drive him in every day and park in the side lot. The lot was usually reserved for teachers, but they let it slide. There was a side door, but Jack liked to hold my hand and walk around the front sidewalk through the main entrance, then down the hall to the special-needs room. We live in Oregon, so most of those days would have been overcast with a good chance of rain, but for some reason, my memory paints those little strolls in warm sunlight.

I remember this one morning when a little boy I'd

never met joined us in our walk toward the classroom and began chatting us up. He had the most delightful lisp. Jack laughed at something, and the boy said, "He'sh alwaysh sho happy." And it made me smile, because at least on this day, with this one boy, my son had a reputation that had nothing to do with disability.

A lot of students tried to talk to him in those days, even though he didn't give them much in return. We were thankful they kept trying. On a good day, he might open and close his hand in their general direction in something almost resembling a wave.

Back at home, we tried to engage him, too, but we didn't get much further than his classmates. Sometimes he let us play tickle games, but beyond that, most of his interaction was food related. We still considered him "nonverbal" even though he had a handful of words and phrases that he employed when he would remember them. He usually didn't. We taught him requests like "water, please" hundreds of times, but they wouldn't stick. One day he would have the phrase, and the next it would be totally new and foreign. And even the words *Mommy* and *Daddy*, when he finally learned them, were purely practical. If he needed water or a snack, he might say our names, but he would probably just point.

While I was thankful for the little gains he had made, they seemed mostly empty. I wasn't all that interested in utilitarian language or the ABCs. We were still bankrupt in the arena that mattered the most: relationship.

In the long debate about whether autism is a blessing or a hindrance, I could never get past that one metric. For me, it was the only one that mattered. How could autism be a blessing from God when it made relationship all but impossible? After all, relationship is our image-of-God inheritance. We are personal beings only because our Dad is a personal Being. Our insatiable desire for relationship is woven into our cells. This is the very purpose for which he created us. And tell me, why would God create us for a purpose, then deliberately block us from accomplishing it?

James, the brother of Jesus, said, "Every good and perfect gift is from above" (James 1:17, NIV), but he said nothing of the hard gifts. As I mentioned earlier, I didn't believe that every situation came flowing from the hand of God. If realities such as sickness, sadness, and disease were his idea, then why did Jesus spend his life and ministry opposing them? If God's will was being done perfectly on earth already, then why did Jesus insist we pray God's will would be done "on earth as it is in heaven" (Matthew 6:10)? It didn't make sense to assume that every trial was his idea—not when he came to redeem those trials.

It might have been different if Jack's symptoms had been milder, but the way I saw it, this disorder was teasing us. Autism was holding my son just out of reach—a carrot on a string. I would have traded much harsher symptoms for a single conversation. A gift from God? Jack was, without question. But his autism?

"I don't care about anything else. I just want to know

him," I would say to Joshua just before I fell apart again. And it was true. Every other desire bowed to that one. Dreams of backyard sports, of college graduations and marriage vows, paled in comparison. The questions that swirled through my mind weren't so much *Why, God?* or *What will we do about his future?* Not anymore. Now I asked things like "What are you thinking about when you flap your socks?" "What scared you so much in your dreams last night?" "Why do you cling so hard to the orange-striped shirt?" and "What is it with you and your living room shrine to Bush's Baked Beans?"

That last one was a question our guests asked us too. There was a small mountain of deep-bronze-colored cylinders growing on the cabinet below our television. It was an ever-shifting pyramid of bean cans. Jack knew all the flavor variations and stacked them accordingly. He would earn new cans by doing enough chores to fill up his sticker chart. The minute he had enough stickers, he would pull us out the door toward the grocery store. We have a great picture of him sitting on the floor of Safeway, staring at all the choices. It took him a half hour to make his pick. The best part? He never opened any of those cans. He doesn't even like beans.

Those quirks didn't make our life harder. We found them delightful, to be honest. But it made us long all the more for an explanation. We wanted to be in on the joke, but he could not bring us there.

We tried to flap next to him sometimes, hoping it might

jog something in him. We thought maybe he would stop, look at us in puzzlement, then let loose a torrent of excited speech about our newly shared affinity. He never did.

So we went on our walks, and we watched his movies, and we tried to involve him in our dance parties, all the while talking to him as if he would understand every word. "Do you know how much I love you, boy?" I would say as I held his hand. He would just look over my head and mumble a line from *Kung Fu Panda*, and my heart would slip down again just a little. In those moments, I would remind his Creator, "Remember, you made him for relationship."

It was during this season that I began to blog in earnest. It's strange to think, now, how it happened. I wanted to start a site that might help grow a following for fiction. But one day I decided to write a little blurb called "Why No, My Son Is Not Rain Man,"[1] and people actually seemed interested, which was a change. Nobody cared much about my fiction.

So I wrote another one called "Fighting Autism with Lame Theology," in which I took on that wonderfully trite Christian phrase "God never gives you anything you can't handle." Soon, it was "50 First Dates with My Autistic Son," a reference to the Adam Sandler movie in which the leading lady had a memory condition requiring her to learn the same information day after day after day, just like Jack.

My close friends shared those articles a little bit on social media, but the bigger reason I kept writing was because I found it strangely cathartic. I didn't keep a journal, and that is basically what the blog became. It not only gave me an outlet to process my experiences with Jack but also provided a map for me to chart that journey, one pushpin at a time. I wanted to remember. No, it was more than that: I wanted to choose what I would remember.

For the first eighteen months of that journal, I wrote about my own progress, partly because I really was making progress, and partly because Jack didn't seem to be making any. Which brings me back to my wife at the pizzeria.

"He is making gains. You're just not seeing them," she had said.

And fine, yes. It was good that he had learned his ABCs, but he learned them in a song. I didn't think that counted for much. After all, my oldest daughter Emily learned the Greek alphabet at eighteen months because we put it to the tune of "Itsy-Bitsy Spider." A kid can memorize anything if you put it to a song. So what did it matter that Jack had learned his letters? It wasn't like he knew how to use them. That hardly seemed like a gain.

There was more than that, though. There was smaller, more daily stuff. When Sara saw Jack going about his life in his own unique way, she would ascribe meaning to it all. He spent much of his time rambling on and on in his garbled speech, quoting his favorite movies. We knew they were quotes because he could get the tone right even if his consonants were all wrong. I saw no rhyme or reason to his use of those quotes. To me, it was just one of those things he did. Sara, however, saw it as something more.

For instance, when Jack would let the water out of his bath, the whirlpool would begin around the drain and he would stand up and shriek, "Daddy, help me!" Sara and I agreed those weren't his own words. They came from a scene in *Finding Nemo*, when the young clown fish is in danger. The whirlpool effect obviously triggered that memory, and Jack was obviously just reliving the scene. I was sure that's all it was. Sara, though, insisted it signaled a growth in his communication: "I think he's using the quote to tell us he's afraid."

All throughout the year, she kept playing that same song: "Treat everything as communication." I was all up for presuming competence, but this was a bridge too far for me. There was absolutely no way to prove that "Daddy, help me!" meant he was scared of getting sucked down the drain. Yes, I know kids actually do fear getting sucked down drains, just like they fear that all their blood will spill out of their bodies when they scrape their knees. But why assume a movie quote is anything more than a movie quote?

And what would it matter even if she was right? That would still be far from an actual conversation. It was hardly an answer to my prayers for a real give-and-take relationship.

Yet . . . hadn't the book of James assured me that "every good and perfect gift" comes from above? And if that were true, wouldn't this hint of relationship, this fragment of connection, however tenuous and hard to believe, qualify as a "good gift"? Because according to that verse in the book of James, it isn't just the perfect gifts that come from above. The good ones do too.

I wonder how many times we dismiss good victories in absence of the perfect ones. In the Land of Unanswered Prayer, most of us aren't crying out for movie quotes that may or may not have some small link to the real world. No, we're pummeling heaven for that one big answer. We focus our timid petitions on the singular, looming giant that casts its shadow on our life: The cancer that keeps coming back, or the family member who refuses to come home. The violent cycle of addiction, rehab, and relapse.

So with every head bowed and every eye closed, we push God toward that one grim, looming impossibility, whatever it may be, for we know that even the impossible is within his reach. We ask and keep on asking. We knock and keep on knocking. We call out from his doorstep, "Lord, let it happen, we pray. Please, open up!" We want God to step out of heaven, come down personally, and set those things right. He split the Red Sea once. He can do it again! Not on Restoration Day—now!

But those big-miracle prayers require an enormous amount of staying power. They sap our spiritual energy like nothing else can. It's easy to pray on and on and on that God would split the sea as long as you're sitting on the dry land, but we happen to be swimming in the midst of these great troubles. We can tread water for a while, but pretty soon, if the waves keep rolling as they are, we will want to give up. And many, many people do. They stop believing in miracles, not because they don't want to believe, but because they are just too tired.

What would happen, though, if we gave our hearts a break from that one big miracle? What if we began to actively pray and look for smaller graces day by day? What if we reached our toes down to the seabed and realized we were swimming over a sandbar? Then we could stand in the water and breathe easy, if only for a while. And who knows? We might even be able to take a few steps while we're at it—forward, toward breakthrough.

The truth is, man cannot live by miracle alone. God works in big ways and small ways. We must learn to see and receive his subtler miracles—his daily blessings— because that is where he does most of his best work.

When Elijah stood on Mount Horeb, God brought the depressed and possibly suicidal prophet out to demonstrate his wonders (see 1 Kings 19:1-13). He showed the prophet a mighty gale that tore the mountainside. He showed him an earthquake that shook the desert. He showed him fire that charred the trees. But the author makes it clear: God was not in any of those wonders. He was in what came next: a whisper.

When the world turns against us, we begin to cry out for the pyrotechnics of heaven: a path through the Red Sea, a falling ball of fire on Mount Carmel—we want the sun to go backward and Lazarus to rise.[2] But most of the time we don't get those displays. We get simpler gifts: a night of unbroken sleep, an unexpected letter, a reprieve from the symptoms. What we get are whispers into our dark and hopeless void; whispers that hover above the face of our unsplit seas; whispers from the lips of God, saying, "Let there be light."

And there is light.

We might not see it at first. We might have to wash the sleep out of our eyes. We might have to train ourselves to see the shadowy forms moving under relative darkness. But when we do, we will find them: unmistakable rays of gold.

Small victories are not completed miracles, but who cares? They are our water in the wilderness, our oases in the Land of Unanswered Prayer, our rest stops along the journey. We would do well to accept them for what they are, for every one of them has been prepared by God himself. Every one. "Every good and perfect gift . . ."

This is what Sara meant when she told me I was missing Jack's gains. I was so focused on the big, grand miracle—the one that would eventually come on Restoration Day—that I was overlooking God's wayside provisions. Jack was moving toward us, and I was missing it.

Then came a moment where I could deny it no longer.

It happened just a few weeks before Jack's eighth birthday, when he tried to steal a book from the school library. He didn't know any better, of course, but we thought it was funny that he tried to smuggle it into his backpack.

He didn't usually have much interest in books, but this time was different. He was eager to bring it home. His teachers said, "It's okay. You can check that book out. Go ahead."

It was a red board book with the title *I Like It When . . .* It was obviously intended for smaller kids—two-year-olds, probably—and it featured two penguins on every page spread. When Jack came home, he was excited to pull it from his backpack.

Sara texted me about it in the middle of the day. Honestly, she was almost frantic. "You've got to see this," she said. I could hardly wait to get done with work.

When I got home, he was still there, lying on his bunk bed, legs crossed in the air and book open in his lap. He wore a massive grin.

"Tell him, Jack," Sara said.

I came in close.

He turned it back to the front page. There was a big penguin and a little penguin, and they were walking together with their fins touching. The words read, "I like it when you hold my hand."

My boy touched the little penguin, then the big one. He met my eyes and said three crisp words that stole my breath: "Jack and Daddy!"

In retrospect, I should have taken off my shoes. It was a holy moment.

Every page had a new scenario. "I like it when you tickle me." "I like it when we splash about." "I like it when you dance with me." At each turn, he tapped the two main characters and said the same thing: "Jack and Daddy."

Of course, I was a wreck by page two. I was bawling. It wasn't just the words or the joy in his laughing face; it was the fact that God had heard my prayer and answered me. Jack saw us. He saw the sum of him and me. He saw our life together, and he knew what it added up to: relationship.

This was nothing short of a revelation. Up until that time, Jack had not used this kind of conceptual language. And now, here he was employing speech on that higher plane, and for such a high purpose. It was a brand-new day. At last, after a long, midnight hunt, we had finally found our prized stag; we had finally caught a "breakthrough."

The penguin incident struck my heart without warning, "like lightning from a clear sky,"[3] to steal a phrase from C. S. Lewis. That single crash reverberated through my world. It jolted me upright and awake. More awake than ever.

But to Sara, this was not lightning from a clear sky, but lightning from a downpour. It was a breakthrough, yes, but not an inexplicable one. Rather, it all made perfect sense to her. She had seen it. She had watched Jack's progression. She had been drinking from the wayside water fountains and believed. She had unwrapped the daily gifts and allowed them to refresh her.

"Jack and Daddy" wasn't a perfect gift, but it was, at minimum, magnificent. It was the kind of gift that we wait years for.

And this is exactly why such milestones are insufficient to sustain us. We aren't supposed to go years without a party. If we want to taste joy and keep on tasting it, we would do well to sharpen our observational skills and begin practicing the art of small-scale celebration.

Sara had been right to suspect Jack was trying to communicate with us. When Jack found those words, I found there was far more to celebrate than I had ever realized. But this is just the way life works with a God who is both invisible and inexhaustible. When we actively look for his hand in our circumstances, a funny thing happens: We start to see it.

CHAPTER 9

"I Am with You"

IN THE MONTHS following the penguin incident, we experienced a string of victories. One of them was simple but profound. It happened in the morning, as I was grabbing my computer bag and about to head out the door. I walked past Jack, who was aware of my routine by now, and he reached up, unbidden, to offer me a kiss.

"I wuv you, Daddy," he said. I almost fell on the floor. It was one of those things I'd always longed to hear from him, and just like that, he said it, turned around, and went about his day. It was awesome.

Then came something more surprising. Sara and I were sharing a lunch with Joshua and his wife, Karen, when we both received a video from Jack's teacher's aide, a delightful woman we called "Mrs. E." She knew our boy inside and out, having worked with him for a few years already, and he adored her. She could get things out of him that no one else could.

We opened the video, and Jack was there, standing with his back to a classroom wall.

"Okay, Jack," Mrs. E said, "what school do you go to?"

"Wauwel Ewementawy," he said to the camera.

Sara and I bolted upright. Did he just say . . .

"Good, Jack. And what's your address?" she asked.

He proceeded to give the street name and house number.

"And your phone number?"

The digits came in the same singsongy pattern as the address had. Sara and I just looked at each other and gaped. We already knew Mrs. E was special, but we didn't know she was a miracle worker.

"What are your sisters' names?"

"Jenna and Emiwy."

"And what are your brothers' names?"

"Sam and Nafan."

The video ended, and I think we all four started laughing. It was absurd. I mean, he had memorized these answers, obviously. This wasn't a breakthrough in heart-level communication, but it was hugely promising, still.

We gave him the same quiz over and over again in the following weeks. He got tired of it too. We could tell, because he started to change the answers. When we asked him the names of his sisters, he grinned and said, "Sam and Nafan." This time, we were in on the joke.

Those strings of small victories put us all in a very hopeful state. Jack seemed to be maintaining his gains for a change, and I was doing better too. Joy was coming to me easier now. I didn't have to work so hard for it, and the sadness, when it came, didn't smother me like before.

But joy, as I said, needs tending, and the hike toward wholeness is rife with detours. In the early autumn of 2014, we hit a detour: Jack had another regression. A big one. In fact, I'd say it was the most drastic step backward that he had experienced since the first one that started it all.

In the past, when a regression came, Jack would forget what he had learned. His vocabulary would vanish, as would his advances in social interaction. He would stand and stare through us, not unwilling but uncertain how to engage with the people he loved. Insomnia would often come roaring back at times like this, too, putting cracks in his calm and making every daily task twice as difficult.

This new regression included all of these symptoms, but with one new wrinkle. He would get upset at something small at first—a movie we wouldn't let him watch or a trigger word someone had accidentally tripped over. Within minutes, though, he would unravel onto the floor, rolling and screeching in a puzzling anguish.

The family would rush in and try our best to console him. We would pull him onto our laps and whisper his favorite words. We would grab the iPad and put on his preferred song (at the time, it was something from *Pocahontas*, I think). We would do everything we could, but it still wasn't enough. He would escape our grasp.

Then came the worst part. He would run to the wall and begin banging his head against it, all the while punching himself with closed fists.

We had, of course, talked with other parents about their experiences with self-injurious behavior, but we had never actually experienced it ourselves. It had sounded like the most demoralizing experience in the world. Turns out, it really was.

All we could do was wrap him up tight and hold his arms close. All we could do was overpower him in an attempt to keep him safe. The screaming would go on and on, sometimes for a few minutes, sometimes for an hour. Always, it was sheer, panicked agony.

Then the dust would settle, and we would wonder what had happened. If we knew what was causing the meltdowns, we could have dealt with them. But he couldn't tell us. Whatever was beneath them—whatever the fears or frustrations or inner disorientation—they held such sway over him that he thought the only way to deal with them was to hurt himself.

We got a helmet for him. They used one at school, too. When the screaming started, we would try to contain him while someone else grabbed the helmet. We would wrestle it onto him until the wave of panic subsided.

I was at a conference in New York on one occasion,

and my wife called me on FaceTime. I hated being gone at this particular time. Tensions were high, and we were both afraid. She brought Jack over to the phone. He had unmistakable bruises all over his forehead. My heart sank.

We were scrambling, Sara and I. What did this mean for Jack's future? He was only eight years old, and the damage he could do was limited, but he was getting older and stronger. His ability to harm himself could only get worse.

I remember talking it over with Joshua and another friend at a pizza place in Times Square. They were great about it, as always. They didn't try to swoop in and fix the problem, for they knew they couldn't. All they did was pray and assure me they would be there for me.

I am richly blessed in the community department. Not everyone is so lucky. Like others who are in the throes of crisis, autism parents often seek comfort from friends, but all too often, they get inspirational platitudes instead. Those platitudes aren't malicious, of course. Just unhelpful.

Here's the most common example, which I mentioned earlier: "God never gives you anything you can't handle."

This phrase is not biblical, despite what people think. It is, at best, a hopelessly flawed paraphrase of 1 Corinthians 10:13, which assures us that God "will not allow [us] to be tempted beyond what [we] are able" (NASB). Paul is giving a straightforward maxim about sin and temptation in that verse, not waxing eloquent about life circumstances. In order to interpret those words in such a way, you have to squint your eyes hard and look through the verse, like one of those magic-eye pictures that haunted shopping malls in the 1990s. No . . . I don't see it either.

Besides the biblical butcher job, I hate the implication that God serves up such hardships like a waiter, carefully delivering only the best tailor-made dishes in life that will correspond to—but never exceed—our appetites. Life is not like that, and we know it.

Hardships often exceed our ability to "handle" them. Consider the little boy who's been raped by his own grandfather; the Somali mother who lost her five children to starvation; the Syrian refugee who just lost not only her family but also her home, city, and heritage. Are such troubles really within the victims' power to overcome?

As extreme as these examples might sound, they aren't so far out of our reach. The reason people turn to drugs, to alcohol, and to suicide is often precisely because they cannot handle the difficulties that have come their way. In this world, we will have troubles—remember?

When people in crisis hear, "God never gives you anything you can't handle," they often receive the inverse message: "Why aren't you able to handle this? What is wrong with you?"

Such a phrase could only come from the modern West, where we worship the self above all things. As individuals, we believe we are unique, we are creative, and we can overcome anything. We are strong, we are resilient, and we believe in the enduring power of the human spirit.

And this is exactly our problem.

Remember when Moses stood barefoot at the burning bush? He was wide-eyed and terrified, not so much by what he was seeing—though a fiery bush that is burned but not consumed would be unnerving enough—but by what he was hearing. The flame was emitting a strange voice, and it was telling him this:

> I will send you to Pharaoh, so that you may bring
> My people, the sons of Israel, out of Egypt.
> EXODUS 3:10, NASB

Can you see the face of Moses? His jaw is moving up and down, but no words are coming out. His eyes bounce around in search of something to hide behind, but he knows there is no escape from The Voice.

At last, he finds his words:

> Who am I, that I should go to Pharaoh, and that I
> should bring the sons of Israel out of Egypt?
> EXODUS 3:11, NASB

"Who am I?"

It is tempting for today's Western Christian to try to laugh off the question. Who was Moses? Who indeed! He was the long-lost prince of Egypt—the adopted grandson of the king. The legend of his birth and rise is the stuff of timeless lore. He went to the finest schools and received the best training in all the land. The hopes of a slave nation were pinned to his chest. He was the one they had been waiting for to fulfill the promise of the God of Abraham. Was there anyone in all the world more equipped to do this job?

In this light, we might imagine God rolling his eyes at such a protest. And then we see the shape of a smile forming in the center of the flame. The bright light dims to a softer shade of orange, and the temperature cools to a mild seventy-seven degrees. Then come the words, backed by heaven's best inspirational soundtracks. Angel voices in major keys propel the soft whispers of the Creator God as he says, "It's all you, buddy. You can do this. All you've got to do is believe in yourself. After all, I never give anyone anything he can't handle!"

That's not how God answers, of course, but follow the scenario out one more step. How does Moses feel when he hears those fictitious words?

It might be just the thing, I suppose. After all, any sports movie worth its salt hinges on such motivational speeches. Moses might, like a high school linebacker, grit his teeth, jump to his feet, and sound his barbaric yawp.

I don't think that's quite right, though. There is nothing in this passage that would indicate Moses is fishing for a compliment or a little pick-me-up. He seems legitimately distressed.

No, I don't think he reacts well. I think he gets even more anxious. You know why? Because he has a good head on his shoulders, that's why. Halftime speeches are flimsy when you know you're outmatched.

Yeah, sure, Moses had been the golden boy once, but that was a long, long time ago. In the subsequent decades, he has been living the life of a Bedouin shepherd. Even if anyone could remember him back home, it wouldn't help him much. The Hebrews would likely view him as a failure, and the Egyptians knew him as a fugitive. He has no assets, no connections, and even his language skills have deteriorated so much that he needs a middleman who can better communicate to the world around him. Indeed, many scholars have suggested that his brother, Aaron, might have served more as a translator than as a spokesperson.

When Moses finally asks, "Who am I?" he doesn't want a pep talk. He wants an escape.

I know how he feels. You probably do too. Sometimes we don't need encouragement as much as we need a reality check. Sometimes our fears tower around us, and we just want people to understand what is happening. We're not looking for pity; we're looking for deliverance.

Jack's severe regression forced me there, next to my old friend Moses. We stand together without shoes, feeling helpless and misunderstood. Who are we to tackle these circumstances? Why would God give such missions to us?

Many people have told me, "God knew what he was doing when he put Jack with you." It's a compliment, I know, and sometimes, when skies are clear, I can almost agree. But then the storm starts all over again, and all I can do is shake my head. Do people think I know how to deal with these new developments? Do they think I have the key to disarming his self-injury and panic attacks? Does my family have an unlimited supply of strength to make it through the long bouts of sleeplessness, and the emotional capacity to ride the swells and regressions of hope and despair?

The Land of Unanswered Prayer can be a confounding place when the flood waters come. The conditions are too harsh, and I'm not strong enough to stand, let alone to navigate my way out of it. I'm not convinced you can either.

I understand that sounds demotivating, but hear me out. The Bible is not a modern Western document. Rather than telling us we are invincible, Scripture continually stresses the opposite: As individuals, we are frail. Heartache abounds far above inspirational anecdotes because human weaknesses abound far above our ability to overcome them.

The human spirit is futile, feeble, and flawed. "The heart is deceitful above all things," Jeremiah 17:9 says. And even when human spirits are willing, human flesh is often weak (see Mark 14:38).

I'm not saying we have no strength. We do. I'm not saying we aren't resilient. We are. I'm just saying we don't have enough resilience to do any of this on our own.

Moses was all too aware of those facts, but he misunderstood the situation. He didn't realize what God was actually saying.

Who am I that I should go to Pharaoh, and that I
should bring the children of Israel out of Egypt?

EXODUS 3:11

Now note God's glorious response:

I will certainly be with you.

EXODUS 3:12

Does God answer the question? No. He shrugs it off.
Who is Moses? That's beside the point. This has almost
nothing to do with Moses. The answer is God himself. In
his presence, the strength comes.

Moses keeps looking for a loophole in this conversation, but each time, God tells him the same thing: "I will
certainly be with you." God didn't pick Moses on the basis
of his competence. No. The only reason this washout shepherd can face a mighty king is because a mightier King
walks beside him.

That King walks with us, too. How else could we
world-weary saints of earth stand against the floods of hell
and circumstance?

"I will certainly be with you."

God reiterates this theme throughout both the Old and
New Testaments. The pages of Scripture are soaked with
the assurance of God's presence. Look, for example, at what
he says to Isaac:

I am the God of Abraham your father. Fear not, for
I am with you and will bless you and multiply your
offspring for my servant Abraham's sake.

GENESIS 26:24, ESV

His presence, God says, is grounds enough not to fear.
He says something similar when he commissions Joshua on
his impossible quest:

Be strong and courageous, for you shall bring the
sons of Israel into the land which I swore to them,
and I will be with you.

DEUTERONOMY 31:23, NASB

. . . and to Gideon on his:

"Please, Lord, how can I save Israel? Behold, my clan
is the weakest in Manasseh, and I am the least in my
father's house." And the LORD said to him, "But I
will be with you."

JUDGES 6:15-16, ESV

You see? There is no arguing with God when he gets like
this. He simply insists on putting the weight of the world
on his own shoulders, not yours. He promises to hold
us tight and see us through, as he did to Isaiah and all of
Israel:

Fear not, for I am with you;
    be not dismayed, for I am your God;
I will strengthen you, I will help you,
    I will uphold you with my righteous right hand.

ISAIAH 41:10, ESV

Fear not, for I have redeemed you;
    I have called you by name, you are mine.
When you pass through the waters, I will be with you;
    and through the rivers, they shall not overwhelm you.

ISAIAH 43:1-2, ESV

The violence of the trial won't affect the outcome. God will not change his mind based on the severity of the flood. He has decided he will be with us, and that is that. His language on the matter is unmistakable:

I will never leave you nor forsake you.

HEBREWS 13:5

And isn't this the very reason Christ came to earth in the first place? Didn't he come in order to be near us? Jesus walked with his disciples, and even when he left, he assured them, "I am with you always, to the end of the age" (Matthew 28:20, ESV). And even when the end of the age arrives, he will take us to his Father's mansion, where we will dwell with him forever (see John 14:1-2).

Even the name of God trumpets the same message.

He is called Immanuel, which means, "God with us" (Matthew 1:23).

"I will be with you" isn't just a promise. It is *the* promise. It is both the rationale of the Abrahamic covenant and the goal of God's great rescue mission. For what did he save us from if not our self-sufficiency?

It is a humbling thing to realize we cannot rescue ourselves, but oh, what a relieving confession it is! We never had the strength to live apart from God anyway. Deep down, we know that. It is a foundational truth of Christianity. It is the reason we came to the cross in the first place; we realized it was destructive to run from our Creator. It was foolish to live apart from him.

None of that has changed. We are still helpless without him. The rising tides will overcome us if we traverse them by ourselves. Whenever we try, we end up feeling powerless and spent. This should come as no surprise. After all, there is nothing more exhausting than the marathon charade of self-assurance. We are not enough. We need our Father.

"Where was God when I was hurt?" we ask. It is a common refrain of the broken. "Where were you, God?"

"Immanuel" is the answer. He has not been hovering above, watching from an alternate dimension of a distant realm. He's been right here in our place of pain. He does not receive our crumpled prayers from the satchels of messenger angels. That might do it for Zeus or Horus or some other ancient god of lore, but not for "God with us." He hears our prayers firsthand because he's right next to us.

God doesn't merely know about our pains—he enters head-long into our war zones and feels all the things we feel.

In his wonderful book *Letters from a Skeptic*, theologian Gregory A. Boyd tells of a time in his university experience when he considered giving up on his faith. He wasn't sure whether he could even believe in God anymore. Like millions of others, Boyd found himself torn between the beauty of creation and the presence of suffering; the grandeur of the night sky and the fires of Auschwitz. There must be a God, but how can there be a God?

One night, he broke down. "Finally," Boyd says, "I looked up to the sky and cried out with a loud, angry voice—'The only God I can believe in is one who knows firsthand what it's like to be a Jewish child buried alive, and knows what it's like to be a Jewish mother watching her child be buried!' And just then it occurred to me (or was it revealed?): That is *exactly* the kind of God Christianity proclaims."[1]

Immanuel. *I was with you. I am with you. I will be with you.*

The week I saw Jack's bruises via FaceTime, I had to fly home and preach a sermon. I preached on Moses at the burning bush. I stood before two hundred faces, and all the feelings were rushing to the surface, invading every sentence I spoke. From behind the pulpit, I read a letter I had written to God the day before. Here are the closing words:

Dear God . . .
I am afraid . . .

135

I have always believed the world is broken, and that you didn't break it. That you are the Great Restorer. That your Son came to make all things new. This has been my conclusion after years of study and thought, but I have to admit, I am biased on this point, because I desperately want to believe it. I need to believe that you are truly, wholly good. That you don't desire innocent children to live frantic and bruised. That you don't lock up a boy's future behind impaired speech centers in the brain.

I don't know how to help my son, and I don't know how to pray. I can't just pray "heal my son" because I don't even know what that means anymore. I don't know what anything means.

So I won't pray anything too bold for now. Instead, I will just remind you that your name is Immanuel, which means "God with us." Come close, Immanuel. Prince of Peace, draw near to my son, and give him rest.

Amen.

By the end of the morning, I was cut to ribbons on stage. The worship team was singing a sweet song about the nearness of God, and I stood in front of them all, hemmed in by two of our church elders who had snuck up on stage to symbolically lift my hands to the air as if I really were Moses. It was a moment of naked surrender. Through supreme weakness, I found sweet relief.

God did not take away Jack's meltdowns that morning, but he heard my prayers. We began to feel his presence in a deeper, more personal way. When Jack's anxiety would flare up and he would begin to hit himself, we wrapped him up with our arms and whispered our assurances into his ear: "We are here. We are with you. We will always love you." And while we wrapped our arms around him, Immanuel wrapped his own around all of us: "I AM here. I AM with you. I will always love you."

Within a few weeks, Jack's self-injuring behavior had subsided, and we were finally able to put the helmet away, back in the attic.

This is the joy I found in the midst of Jack's regressive detour. It wasn't the stuff of dance parties after a mighty breakthrough. It was the quiet joy of a man who realized he would never have to walk by himself—the sweet relief of a lost sheep who had been found.

For the Lord truly is our shepherd. He bids us to lie down in patches of green. He restores our broken souls, taking us all the way from still waters to the Valley of the Shadow, to enemy-occupied territory. There we find a most unlikely sight: a banquet table, set right in the very midst of our trials, our sadnesses, our regressions. An audacious table in the presence of our enemies.

We see the whites of their eyes as they peer out at us from behind the bushes. We see the spears in their hands and the hatred in their faces. And still we feast without fear, for he is with us. We take seats near the head of the table, filling our goblets with wine. We revel in his goodness; we glory in his songs.

"I am with you" means we never have to walk alone. That is reason enough for joy. There is no need, friend, to wait for an uptick in circumstances. There is no reason to fast until the floodwaters subside. No matter how high the waters rise, the God of Moses carries us on his shoulders. In our weaknesses, he is strong. And since we walk with him, he makes us strong too.

CHAPTER 10

To Give Him a Superpower

"ONCE UPON A TIME there were three brothers: Jack, and Sam, and Nathan. And they had superpowers."

Jack was lying on the top bunk, fiddling with his favorite toy, while the younger two sat below, wide-eyed and waiting. This was one of their favorite parts of the day.

"What were their superpowers, Dad?" Sam asked.

Sam was probably six at the time—three years younger than Jack; but in many ways, he is the oldest brother. He's the responsible one of the bunch—the protector and leader. This was an easy one.

"Sam had superstrength and indestructibility," I said. He grinned. It was exactly what he wanted.

Dealing out superpowers for a children's story is easy

enough. The key is to take a characteristic the child already possesses and then maximize it. If a kid is a show-off, for instance, you can't give him invisibility, even if he asks for it. That would be nothing short of storytelling malpractice. Give him Lightning Power, or flame-throwing fists, or even a generic Iron Man suit—anything that helps him show off. If he's a pocket comedian, please don't give him flying power, because there's nothing funny about flight. Give him something like Endless Banana Peel Power, or anything with "Underpants" in the title.

Three-year-old Nathan fit that latter category, but he was also a bit of a brute. Thus, I gave him Tackle Power, the ability to deliver an epic thumping to anyone or anything he wanted. Both younger boys whooped and laughed at that announcement. They saw the comic potential at once, and Nathan gloried in it.

Then Sam asked the inevitable question I had been avoiding: "Dad, what's Jack's superpower?"

It doesn't sound like a serious consideration, I know, but it felt a little heavy. It had implications. Stories are powerful things.

Our family has always been a story family. It was only fitting, then, that the "Jack and Daddy" breakthrough happened with the help of a book. Ever since my daughters, Emily and Jenna, were just knee-high pixies, we were either reading books aloud or creating our own family mythology. We invented Teddy and Marianne, the child jockeys who could speak to the secret monkeys of the forest; Cowboy

Pete and his fast-talking deputy, Rocky Raccoon; Ricky the Ostrich and his magnificent submarine; and Zach and Zoe the kangaroos, whose popular comic circus act consisted only of cheeky comments and pies to the face.

These weren't good stories by any grown-up measure, but the kids liked them, both because I made them a part of the story and because I did funny voices.

But there was a less obvious factor that increased the potency of our bedtime routine: Stories create culture. They become centerpieces around which people gather. They become part of our psyches. Stories build community, and communities—good ones, anyway—can become conduits for celebration.

My celebration muscles were atrophied at the time of the penguin incident. In my search for joy, I had to learn not only how to see small victories but also how to savor them. This is extremely difficult to do by yourself. Celebration is meant to be shared.

Sharing had been an easy thing for me back when I was in my twenties. I used to love surrounding myself with friends, and when I was alone, I hated the feeling that I might be missing out on something. Our house was always full of guests. We played music and board games. We watched movies and football. We had rhythms of feasting and laughter.

None of that was true anymore, though. Somewhere along my journey through the wilderness, I had lost my thirst for companionship. This seems fairly common for people in their thirties and forties, from what I can tell. As our life experiences stack up, our youthful idealism loses its conviction, and many of us tend to withdraw. It doesn't take an autism diagnosis to make that happen; all it takes is a little disappointment.

It's not that I didn't have friends at that time—I did. I just didn't call them very often. I preferred to do my work, then stay home with my family, as if I didn't need anyone else.

Ironically, it was in those homebound evenings that my children showed me the power of both community and celebration. One memory sticks out above the rest.

Picture this: All three little boys are in the bathtub. Sam is sitting on the edge, reenacting a scene from *Ratatouille,* one of Jack's favorite movies. Sam is playing the part of Linguini, who is supposed to throw Remy the rat into the river; but he can't bring himself to do it.

"I can't cook, can I?" Sam says to his oversized bottle of shampoo, his stand-in for the jar that holds the rat prisoner. "But you . . . you can, right? Look, don't be so modest—you're a rat, for Pete's sake!"[1]

Jack is watching it all with silent glee, and Nathan's face is full of anticipation. His part is coming up.

Sam puts his hands on the bottle and hesitates just like Linguini, who wants to set his little rat friend free so he can help him cook, but is afraid the little guy might run away. It is a terrific piece of filmmaking, but the bathtub version is way funnier.

Little Nathan sees his cue. He climbs out of the tub and gets down on his hands and knees, soaking wet and ready for action.

"Okay, I'm gonna let you out now," Sam says to the shampoo. "But we're together on this, right? Okay . . ."

The moment he picks up the bottle, Nathan becomes the rat, waddling out of the room at breakneck speed, leaving a wide trail of bathwater in his wake. The bathroom echoes with laughter. If you've never seen a stark-naked three-year-old impersonating a rodent chef from Paris, you haven't seen anything.

By far the best part of the memory, though, is the joy in Jack's eyes. He's been drinking in every moment. He knows the movie even better than his brothers do, and here, in the middle of a mundane cleaning, it has come to life. Sam and Nathan put on their elaborate little play for one reason only: They know it will make him happy.

The memory reminds me of what God said in Genesis: "It is not good that man should be alone" (2:18). The fact that he was about to give Adam a wife should not narrow the application of this statement. It's not a verse for weddings but a verse for humans. Human beings are not meant to be alone; we are hardwired for relationship. Those with disabilities are not exceptions. It is not good for Jack to be alone—he needs his brothers.

Pastors like me often forget to emphasize brotherly love. We talk plenty about the love of God our Father (*agape* in the Greek). That is appropriate, since it all begins with the ever-sustaining, never-failing love of our Father. And we talk about romantic or sexual love too (*eros*), since family plays such a vital role in each of our lives. We often overlook a third kind of love, however: the essential love of friends and comrades (*phileo*). I'm not really sure why that happens. Maybe it's because *phileo* is so out of fashion in so many places.

In the world of Western social media and culture, friendship looks like nothing more than a "plan b" of *eros*. We make jokes about the dreaded "friend zone," in which a would-be romantic interest is demoted to the sad and lowly place of a mere platonic mortal, and we castigate heartfelt friendships, relegating them to the realm of "bromances." In either case, the highest form of love is assumed to be the romantic, sexual kind. Friendship is a downgrade, or worse, a punch line.

When I look at my kids, though, and the way they rally around Jack, I am reminded again how misguided this kind of thinking is. *Phileo* holds greater power than *eros* ever could. It has the potential not only to give joy but also to bestow a precious sense of belonging. Communities only exist because brotherly love exists.

When Sam memorizes long swaths of Jack's favorite movie dialogue just to see him smile, he is telling his brother, "I care about the things you care about."

When Jenna visits Jack's school to share a wordless lunch with him in the cafeteria, she is telling him, "You matter to me."

When Emily wraps her arms around Jack in the throes of an anxious meltdown, she is telling him, "We will not reject you. Ever."

And when Nathan, the youngest, gets behind Jack's bike—training wheels and all—and gives him a running push, he is making a promise about his future: "You won't have to go it alone."

This is not only what siblings do—this is also what friends do. I'm not talking about the dude you lift with at the gym or the essential oils guru you talk to online. I mean the people who have no illusions about what kind of person you are. I mean those who make an honest effort to understand you—people who know how stubborn you can be but still want to hang out. They know your flashes of temper and your tendency toward jealousy. They have seen you at your most pathetic, but they haven't run away. They don't excuse your many flaws, but neither do they make ultimatums.

Those relationships are supposed to be support beams that lift us over floodwaters. And yet in the early days of my rediscovery of joy, I was still avoiding them.

A couple of years ago, I was speaking to a group of ministry students about the need to become vulnerable with one another in the church. One student in the back of the class raised her hand. She had been friendly and upbeat the entire morning, but now her face was pure ice.

"Why?" she demanded.

"Why what?" I asked.

"Why do I have to open up to other people? Why can't it just be me and God?"

I wish I would have taken more time to measure my response, but I wasn't thinking and let the words fly.

"Because you're not strong enough on your own," I said. It was true, but perhaps a little too blunt.

She hardly spoke to me for the rest of the week. Clearly, she had history in this arena. She was carrying hurts that had driven her into a numb isolation, but relationship was the thing she needed in order to truly heal.

Why do we run away from the things that can heal us? You've done it, too, I'd wager. We've both slid into desolation when it was easier than communication. We've both curled up on our beds to stare at the blue glow of our phones, scrolling past endless images of glowing families with their seemingly perfect lives, and we've felt our hearts wince. We've plugged in our earbuds to wash away the loneliness with melodies of sad singers or the droning on of talking heads that we don't have to talk back to.

If we continue on like that, our worlds can become private echo chambers where melancholy bounces back and forth, up and down across our hearts without any window of escape. Isolation is a self-made prison. Yes, the food is lousy and the decor is drab, but we lock ourselves in anyway because we think it's easier than the alternative.

And in some ways, it is. Letting other people in is as frustrating as it is difficult. I remember sitting one day with a group of men, trying to verbalize how hard things had been with Jack. I wanted prayer and encouragement, but what I got was advice, and not very good advice either. Their sentiments all flowed from good, compassionate hearts, but none of them knew what it was like in my life. They weren't autism dads, so how could they?

The world probably doesn't understand what you're going through either. How can it? The sickness you're trying to beat, the loss you're reeling from, the separation you're experiencing—nobody feels those things in precisely the same way you're feeling them. "Opening up" often leads to more frustration.

To curb that frustration, many turn to online communities instead. When we're on the internet, we can find "our tribe" of people who are walking parallel paths with us. Social media offers an endless assortment of laser-focused microcommunities where we can rant and rave about how the world "just doesn't get it." But even those connections can quickly descend into jealousy and good old-fashioned bitterness as the commonalities erode. Each one of us carries with us our own complex web of history, genetics, relationships, and circumstances that makes our lives unique. Even those in similar situations cannot, except in a very general sense, ever say, "I know how you feel."

Online relationships are rarely satisfying anyway. There is no substitute for real flesh-and-blood community. The fact remains, though, that real flesh-and-blood community is hard. Relationship is fragile. Even when we're not feeling particularly broken, it requires a price:

energy, grace, and vulnerability. Those costs skyrocket in the Land of Unanswered Prayer. We are on edge in this wilderness. Our energy is sapped much of the time, and we have little left over for kindness, let alone a scary thing like authenticity.

That is why I dove into my isolation back in the days of Jack's diagnosis, and that's why I stayed there for so long. "I'm just not an extrovert anymore," I would say. Even if that was true, it was an obvious oversimplification. The truth is, I just didn't want to make the effort.

"Why don't you go hang out with the guys tonight?" my wife would say, and I would hem and haw about being too tired and not wanting to be around other people. Once again, however, my wife proved wiser than me. She knew the value of friendships. She knew community was a conduit for celebration.

One summer evening, my buddy Robert invited my family and a bunch of other friends to his company's suite at a minor-league baseball game. Jack got excited when the mascot came to visit, but he spent most of the game sitting still in the corner seat of the balcony, watching the action while quietly quoting movies to himself. It all made for an extraordinarily rare stress-free evening. I got to hang out with people who knew us and loved my entire family, and Jack, against all odds, seemed to watch all nine innings with a bit of interest.

It wasn't until the game ended that his OCD kicked into high gear. When we all got up to leave, he bolted out the door and fled down the stairs. Sara chased after him while I collected the rest of our kids.

Inside a minute, the boy was down by the dugout where some players were signing autographs. A pitcher saw him, signed a ball, and handed it to him. But Jack had no interest in souvenirs. He only wanted to do one thing.

So he threw the ball onto the field.

Sara cringed, but the pitcher just laughed and said, "Better let him go get it."

Of course, that wasn't allowed. The grounds crew was already out there, and the field wasn't open to the public. But in a moment, the boy was on the field.

That's when the rest of us saw him.

"Jack's on the field," someone yelled.

When he picked up his ball, he didn't go back to Sara. She started to follow him from a distance, but he was ignoring her and marching straight for the pitcher's mound. The grounds crew pretended not to see him.

The stands were mostly empty by then, but you wouldn't know it. My friends and I unleashed enough whoops to fill the stadium.

"Go, Jack!" we shouted.

He was on a mission, though, and could not be distracted even by his rowdy fans. All night long, he had watched the same thing happen over and over again, probably two hundred times: Somebody would step on the mound and throw the little white ball. For him, it was simple logic. That's what you did at a baseball game.

So that's what he was going to do. He stepped up onto the mound, looked toward the invisible batter, and tossed the ball in the direction of home plate.

We went ballistic. All of us. Even my younger sons cheered through their visceral jealousy. And a moment later, he thew it again. An encore.

It didn't matter that the ball didn't make it halfway to the plate. When he returned to us in the stands, he was nothing less than a sports hero. But like all good heroes, he shrugged off our adulation with the humble satisfaction of a man who had just gone out there and done his job and was ready to hit the showers.

That would have been a nice moment, no matter what. My son, on a baseball diamond? My autistic little boy accidentally engaging in a bit of civil disobedience? Awesome.

But I wasn't the only one who witnessed it. My friends surrounded me and cheered alongside me: Robert and Wendy, Josh and Carlie, Aaron, Hannah, and all the kids. Their presence made it an electrifying victory that I'll never forget, and that is the way it's supposed to be. Celebration is a team sport.

Have you read the parable of the shepherd who loses just one sheep, then leaves his entire flock to find it? He does find it, and when he does, "he joyfully puts it on his shoulders and goes home. Then he calls his friends and neighbors together and says, 'Rejoice with me; I have found my lost sheep'" (Luke 15:5-6, NIV).

The same thing happens with the woman who tears her house apart looking for the money she's lost: "When she finds it, she calls her friends and neighbors together and says, 'Rejoice with me; I have found my lost coin'" (Luke 15:9, NIV).

When the prodigal returned home, his father did not go inside, close his door, and eat a piece of cake all by his lonesome. No, he cried out, "Bring the fattened calf and kill it. Let's have a feast and celebrate" (Luke 15:23, NIV), because that is the only way celebration works.

It doesn't matter the situation. Whether it's a small, insignificant baseball story, a whopping "Jack and Daddy" breakthrough, the momentous return of a son, or a victory so tiny we have to squint to see it, the truth is the same: The joy we find in our wilderness is far too valuable to carry by ourselves.

And so is the aching.

Remember the day I preached about Moses during Jack's regression, and two of our elders held my arms up? Well, something else happened on that morning. When the dust had settled and the congregation was clearing out, I looked down to the front row where two of my good friends stood looking up at me with the red eyes of solidarity. I stepped down, and when they embraced me together, I thought I heard heaven's whisper: "See? I have given you brothers."

And I knew in that moment that my isolation was not paying off and never would pay off. I knew that *phileo* was

worth the awkward journey. It didn't matter that these
friends didn't perfectly understand my pain, because I
couldn't perfectly understand theirs either.

It's an overrated consideration anyway. It might feel
good to rant a bit about about common societal enemies,
but that is a flimsy foundation for a friendship. In fact,
such relationships often end up poisoning wells that are
supposed to refresh us. They quickly become toxic.

In contrast, one of the most potent aspects of a positive
community is the range of experiences and opinions it
offers. Each of us has walked only one path. When we walk
with a friend, though, we inherit new histories—portals
into other worlds.

Sometimes a good world is hard to find. I've been
blessed in this regard. Even though Sara and I have no rela-
tives within two thousand miles, we are not without family.
We have Janae, for one thing. Our show tune–singing
friend moved to Oregon with us and has stuck with us
ever since. She not only encourages our hearts when we're
down but also celebrates the best of times with us: soccer
matches, dance recitals, and late-night games of Ticket to
Ride.

And we have our church family. It's difficult to over-
state how much they have given us. These saints don't just
encourage us after sleepless nights; they also get us laughing through the day. They ask us what we need, and they
try their best to provide it. They lend us faith by sharing
their own rich histories. Sometimes they let us rant when

we're down, but they stop our ranting, too, because there is always hope beyond our present troubles.

This is a peculiar benefit a community of believers can offer: We can always remind one another of the unseen work of Christ in the here and now, and of his eventual return to finish that work. Not all of us do this well, but when we do, there is no support system like it on the planet.

Once we get there, we will discover the power and beauty of interdependence. I can't lift my hands, but your arms are strong. You might be thirsty, but I carry in my canteen the fresh waters of encouragement. Truly, when we meet one another in our humble weaknesses, the breath of the Spirit blows through the in-between country. The hands of Christ become our hands.

This is precisely what Jesus prayed for before he sacrificed himself on our behalf:

> The glory which You have given Me I have given to them, that they may be one, just as We are one; I in them and You in Me, that they may be perfected in unity, so that the world may know that You sent Me, and loved them, even as You have loved Me.
>
> JOHN 17:22-23, NASB

"Dad, what's Jack's superpower?"

I pondered the question. It was a loaded one, the kind of question that could change the way Jack's brothers think about him. The kind of question that could change the way he thinks about himself.

If stories create culture, what kind of culture should we create? In the end, I opted for hope.

"Jack has golden socks, and when he flaps them, a strong wind comes that blows away the bad guys."

The little brothers gaped. "Whoa! Flapping power? Awesome!"

I continued, my mind racing. "Yes, and when he flaps them at the ground, it pushes him high into the air, and he can go wherever he wants to."

"Jack can fly?"

Yes. Jack can fly. And when it's time to rain justice down on the great ice cream capers of Junction City, Super Sam and Tackle Boy Nate will latch on to the shoulders of their big brother, Flap Jack, and together, they will fly high over the trees until they see that particular black pickup truck hightailing it out of town. Because if he could, I believe Jack would do that for his brothers. He would take them anywhere, and he would use his powerful stims to bail them out of their boyish recklessness.

Sam and Nathan need their brother. We need our brothers and sisters too. We cannot walk this path alone. Yes, I know God is there, so we're not alone anyway, and if we were somehow to be marooned on a Pacific rock for ten years, God would surely see us through.

Fortunately, though, in the real world, he has given us people with whom we can share our worst days and our best days, our broken projectors and our penguin incidents. He has not only given *agape* but has also provided means for *phileo*.

I still tell Superbrothers stories. On warm afternoons, I can hear crashing and squealing sounds seeping in from the backyard as Sam and Nathan reenact their adventures from the night before. I open the door a crack and see them running up to their big brother, who is flapping on the porch, lost in his own thoughts as always.

"Hey, Jack, you just saved us! Good job, Flap Jack!"

He eyes them, then turns his back to resume his business, just as they return to theirs. They remain undaunted by his dismissals. Visions of hope will do that, I think. They will make allowances for temporal wincing.

In the end, this is the greatest beauty community can offer. True friends know what it is to embrace without any thought of reciprocation. There is no cost for *phileo*, no fine print, no strings attached. It is a whispered promise: We love you here, and we love you there. We accept you right now, and we'll keep on asking for "strength for today and bright hope for tomorrow," as the hymn says.[2]

Jack needs it. I need it. And you need it.

You cannot do this by yourself, friend, and that's just the way it's supposed to be. Aching joy is meant to be shared.

CHAPTER 11

Slaying Cynicism

AS BEAUTIFUL AS COMMUNITIES ARE, they all tend to have their own blind spots. Sometimes those blind spots are a bit ironic, like with the church that emphasizes grace but cannot smell the rot of legalism growing in its own pews. Or the college that boasts in its diversity, all while cracking down on any view that diverges from its own.

I've been part of the autism blogging community for several years now, and I think we have our own ironic blind spot. We are a tough group of parents. I mean, we put up with a lot of crap that other parents don't face. We sometimes have to stare down teachers and principals and sleepless nights and maddening obsessions. We cope with seizures, diffuse meltdowns, and work for months or years to win battles that normally take days or weeks (think potty training, for instance), and we remain undaunted.

We are tough people. And yet we can also be overly sensitive.

Here's what happens. Someone out there—some parent who holds us in high esteem, usually—will try to give us a pat on the back. She knows we're struggling, so she might say the classic, "God never gives us anything we can't handle," or "I don't know how you do it," or "God knew what he was doing when he gave your son to you." For various reasons (some of which I've already discussed), those comments tend to irritate us, and we sometimes rant about it behind closed doors or in closed Facebook groups. Other times, we let everyone know it by posting snarky memes or writing posts like "Seven Things Y'all Need to Stop Saying to Special-Needs Parents Right Away, K?"

Why do we do it? Many reasons. We are tired all the time, for one thing. But more than that, I think it's because we're like every other demographic online—we have too many windows into too many other lives. People say the internet made the world smaller. They are wrong. The internet made the world larger than we ever dreamed. Every day, it bombards us with reports of floods and fam-ines, explosions and assaults in cities we've never heard of in countries whose names we cannot pronounce. And every day, it tempts us with videos of gourmet meals we could never create at beachside resorts we could never afford. A few swipes is all it takes to see the juxtaposition: Some humans suffer more than they should ever have to, while others thrive in ways we never will.

How do we turn off the comparison machine? How do we get past the differences between us or between the idealistic visions we hold and the realities we face? Our newsfeeds are rife with images of the "normal" family life: epic vacation slideshows from our friends and neighbors, pictures from the softball team, and posts that boast, "Guess who just made the honor roll . . ."

As special-needs families, we know these are worthy life moments to share, but in our weaker days, we can feel the sensitive stab of self-pity. Our lives are different, see, and some of us might never experience those "normal" family moments.

I have some dear friends with a son who is also named Jackson, born the same month and year as my son. Their boy plays basketball, inhales books, and is well versed in the intricacies of the Star Wars universe. He's a delightful kid. And I admit there are some days—more sensitive days—when I look at how grown-up he seems, and how the world is opening up to him by new inches every day, and I can't stop my heart from sinking just a hair.

How strange it is that happy things can tempt us to anguish, and that someone else's good can elicit potential resentment. It is nothing but a blessing for a boy to grow into a young man. But it is hard to partake of those blessings from the outside.

Once again, this is not a problem unique to autism

families. The temptation to envy does not discriminate. Wherever our hearts ache, wherever our sensitivities lie, someone will stumble over them and reawaken our resentments once again. Then we must decide how our hearts will respond.

Around the time of my son's regression into self-injury, a season in which I wasn't feeling particularly blessed, Joshua sat me down and got serious.

"Jason, I want to ask you to preach on something, but you're not going to like it," he said.

I don't remember where we were, but I'll never forget the timing of the conversation. It came just a matter of days after I had blubbered onstage about Jack's struggles.

"Okay?" I said with eyebrows raised in a defensive posture.

"I want you to preach about how God answers prayer."

I winced. In another season, from another person, it might have been a happy topic.

"I know it's not going to be easy, but I think it's right."

I accepted the offer, of course, because it was not really a request—it was an assignment. He's my boss, after all. He might have let me weasel out of it, but I didn't want to let him down. More than that, I agreed with him. This seemed right. There was a tugging in my spirit to face down this topic once and for all.

So I began my preparation by gathering miracle stories stretching back as far as the fathers of my faith. Biblical examples were everywhere, of course. The children of Israel followed God because of the memory of the splitting sea. The crowds from Galilee followed Jesus because they saw him heal the lepers and shush the storms. And the early church overcame and prospered in part because of their testimonies of what the Spirit of Christ had done through them.

The ancient wonders remain as much a part of my heritage as the men who worked them: Moses and Elijah, Peter and Paul, and a hundred others. The entire Christian faith is built on the belief that one Man was raised from the dead. If you remove the miracles from the Scriptures, you reduce the faith to a series of meaningless platitudes.

So I embraced them all. The stories came rushing hard between the banks of the Old and New Testaments, down through the rapids of Christian history. All of it gathered together in a deep reservoir, mixing with the fresher springs of modern testimony: missionary tales of sandwiches multiplying, impossible healings, and visions of angels. These weren't strangers telling such stories; they were my friends.

For the uninitiated, accounts like these can unleash a fresh promise. The idea that there might exist realities beyond the reach of what we can touch or taste, and that those realities can sometimes tear into our realm on the tip of God's finger . . . that is a compelling proposition. It is too much for some to accept, of course, but for those hurting masses who have lost confidence in the material world, it can usher in a new and welcome hope.

But I was not among the uninitiated. As I threw myself down into these accounts of wonder and possibility, I felt no rush of cool comfort. I only felt frustration. If God could break through into our circumstances, why wasn't he doing it now? Why wasn't he breaking through for Jack? Shouldn't the King of the universe at least be fair?

This is the rock where so many of our ships wreck. It's not really about miracles in the end, but about fairness. Equity. You don't have to believe in the supernatural to feel a sense of cosmic wrongness around you. All it takes is a glimpse through someone else's window—someone going through something really bad . . . or really good.

Either condition can arouse a protest:

"Lord, why did you make those people feel such suffering?"

"Lord, why did you bless those other people and not me?"

Some have tried to turn these discussions into mechanical, cause-and-effect relationships. You want to be blessed? Here's how to be blessed: Pray these prayers and pray them this way; follow these steps and walk like me. God will answer your petitions as long as you follow the recipe.

Sometimes, it seems to work. The prayer is answered. The crisis ends, and the relationship heals. The fever passes, and the blessing comes. And when it comes, we think to ourselves, *Maybe it really is that simple! Maybe if I follow this path, I will continue to be blessed!*

Then the other shoe drops. The questions come. The broken thing refuses to be fixed, no matter how loud the praying or how right the living. Suddenly, all those outside assurances start to sour. From then on, it's hard not to bristle at even benign displays of contentment or innocent proclamations of God's generosity toward us.

"You think God's blessed you with that promotion, do you? Well, congratulations on cracking the code."

We treat all of this as if we were the first to have come up with such questions, but even the prophets of old recognized the distinct lack of formula in the cosmic narrative. For them, the most common objection concerning God's fairness seemed to center on the fact that wicked people still received God's blessings. They didn't like the fact that the sun rose on both the evil and the good (see Matthew 5:45). Some of them skirted the issue, but Jeremiah stated his case plainly:

> Righteous are You, O LORD, that I would plead my case
> with You;
> Indeed I would discuss matters of justice with You:
> Why has the way of the wicked prospered?
> Why are all those who deal in treachery at ease?
> JEREMIAH 12:1, NASB

It is only right and good to bring such irritations to God directly. We still have to be honest even after we sing our psalms of lament. The world is complex. Spiritual denial won't help us navigate any of this.

Then again, neither will cynicism.

Cynicism takes a grim posture. It tells us we can't trust

God because he's either arbitrary or loaded down with a busy schedule, and we can't trust life because somehow it's rigged against us. As a result, even life's rewards are flimsy and fleeting.

Truly, cynicism is every bit as destructive as denial, if not more so. It is one of life's most subversive intruders, slipping in through the gate of intellectualism amid the crowd of questions and hiding under the fog of disappointment. If we don't deal with cynicism, it will take command of our hearts and choke out our joy.

But how can we avoid it? We live in the Land of Unanswered Prayer, after all. In this country, giving in to cynicism is like giving in to gravity. It is not only easy but is also the natural pull. Left to our own feelings, we will become cynical. We will despair.

David the psalmist, who had his own long season of unanswered prayer in the wilderness, faced down these questions with even greater intensity than Jeremiah did. He had to hide in his desert for years, waiting for the fulfillment of God's promise. He was a fugitive from his own king—the righteous prey of a deranged lunatic. And yet he did not give in to despair.

I imagine him now, this shepherd warrior, hungry and battle worn, glaring at me across the entrance of his cave. He listens to my troubles. He doesn't minimize them even though he could, by all rights. No, he hears my pains, my frustrations, until my words run out.

"You've gone through far more than I have," I tell him.

"So tell me how can I avoid becoming cynical. How have you kept yourself from despair?"

He inhales deeply, the young poet, and answers me this way:

> I would have despaired unless I had believed that I would see the goodness of the LORD in the land of the living.
>
> PSALM 27:13, NASB

I grimace. It's too simple. David believed he would see God's goodness—not just on Restoration Day, but in this life too. It set him on a mission to find the hand of God.

"But I have prayed, and he has not answered," I respond. "I have been looking, and I don't see the goodness of God!"

David frowns, and I wonder why. My protest is valid, isn't it?

Or maybe it isn't. After all, I had, actually, seen God's good gifts by now. There was the "Jack and Daddy" moment, for one thing, and I had come to know both the firm embrace of community and the abiding presence of my Father.

But it's so easy to forget those blessings. Our hearts can embrace deep truths and then, against all reason, let those truths go. This is why I say hope meanders and joy needs tending. These aren't multiplication facts that we learn once and never forget. These are lessons we must learn again and again until they make their home in the soil of our souls. In this regard, I am a slow learner.

The giant-slayer David eyes me like he sees it all, but he doesn't address my forgetfulness. Instead, he puts his hand on my shoulder like the good commander that he is. His eyes are not harsh, but they are firm: "Jason," he says, "why are you making this all about you?"

And at those imagined words, I remember that every good and perfect gift comes from above. Every single gift is a testament to God's goodness, not just the ones I personally receive.

Truly, God is bigger than my circumstances. That doesn't just mean he can overcome them; it also means that he sits above them in his sprawling, omnipresent majesty. Yes, our trials matter. Jack's panic attacks are real, and they matter, but they are also limited things with a beginning and an end. They are dark clouds in my sky, but they are far too small to define the entire firmament.

The problem with cynicism and despair is that they are not only too sad but also intellectually dishonest. It is blind hubris to suggest that God doesn't answer prayer simply because we ourselves are still waiting for answers. It is a twisted and bankrupt logic that dismisses God's gifts for our neighbors on the grounds that we didn't happen to receive the same gifts ourselves. Cynicism is a rigged, deceptive posture. It affirms every misery while dismissing every joy.

The truth is, we are fortunate to be so small. The sun

does not revolve around us or around today's sadness. Truth does not hinge on the frame where we stand. The rain has fallen, and will still fall, on the just and the unjust alike. And this is good news, friend. The world is big, and history is long, and even when we are waiting for our own breakthroughs, we can still see the goodness of God in the land of the living. Wherever we find God's blessings, we have the opportunity to affirm them. Wherever good news strikes, we can offer hearty amens.

Sometimes it is easy to share in our neighbors' celebrations, but not always. When the family down the street has their fifth baby while you are still childless and barren, it stings. When your neighbor gets the healing you've been crying out for, it stings. When your marriage is on the rocks and you see the latest wedding invitation on the counter, it stings.

Those stabs of resentment come unbidden, I know, but I urge you to resist them. Fight them. For indeed, such testimonies serve as evidence that love can endure the long winters and hope can still grow in dry soil. God is still active, both through invisible wonders and through the hands of his children.

In the meantime, there is a freedom that comes to those who refuse to envy. They not only render powerless the bonds of cynicism and despair but also receive fresh doses of joy. They join the parties that are happening around them.

Celebration, remember, is a team sport. But when Paul said to rejoice with those who rejoice, it wasn't just for the sake of encouraging the person who was already excited. It was also for our sakes—the ones who desperately need reasons to celebrate. We've been waiting, haven't we? Well, here's our chance. Our friends are having parties. It has nothing to do with us, but we can join them and forget ourselves in the music.

I know, I know, this doesn't solve the fairness problem, but who cares? What good has it ever done to keep a tally of blessings and troubles in the first place? Nobody actually wants to live in a world of perfect fairness where everybody gets the same thing. God made us unique, and he gives us unique experiences. This is part of what makes life beautiful. There are different bodies of every size and shape, every color and condition. God spread us out to live in valleys and along bayous and amid great plains, and we experience life inside dense cities and sparse mountain villages and poverty-stricken shantytowns. Everywhere we turn, we see endless varieties of beauty and brokenness.

Remember the parable of the talents? The Master, who represents God, gave some people five talents, some two, and some one (see Matthew 25:14-30). He never was fair in the modern sense, for fairness is concerned only with sameness. But God never has seemed to care much for uniformity. Rather, he is a just God who will never measure us with another person's yardstick. If he has given us much, he will require much. God looks on our individual hearts, and one day, when we stand before him, we will not give an account of our neighbors but of ourselves—what blessings we had, what truths we knew, and whether we, personally, kept the faith (see Luke 12:48; 1 Samuel 16:7; Romans 14:12).

When I finally preached my sermon about the God who answers prayer, I had to lean on mystery the whole time. I never cracked any code to access God's miraculous blessings, and I still didn't know what to do with all the seemingly simple promises regarding healing in the New Testament. It all looked so easy in Scripture: Man prayed and God answered. That bothered me. Sometimes it bothers me still.

But I knew this without a doubt: God was not silent. He might not have been breaking through with a miracle in my life, but he was active in my community. That meant he was still there, and he was still good.

In the previous month alone, we had heard many testimonies of God's faithful intervention among our own ranks. One woman had been healed of hepatitis on the day of her baptism, and another bowed her head after a sermon and was set free from the shackles of extreme vertigo. And as if physical healing weren't enough, another woman had asked God for emotional healing after a lifetime of family guilt. He took it all in an instant. Her heart was free.

I referenced each of these recent instances, then invited anyone who had received a "profound answer to prayer" to stand up. All around the sanctuary, people rose to their feet to bear witness to God's powerful intervention in their lives. How can a soul remain deflated in such a place? Despair cannot bear to lift its head in the presence of God's goodness. A cynic cannot withstand a living, breathing testimony.

I told one last story after that:

In 1961, a Canadian boy fell suddenly, drastically sick, and his parents took him to the hospital. The doctors ran a battery of tests, and when they got the results, it was so bad that no one wanted to tell the boy's mother. The doctors told only his dad. It was leukemia, and the child had only a short time left.

Over the next few weeks, the boy's condition worsened. He stayed in the hospital and grew weaker and weaker while his father called out to God. Soon, the man knew his son was not long for this world, so he closed down his mechanic shop for three days while he prayed and fasted with desperation.

Then he went back to the hospital. His son was sitting up and moving, somehow feeling amazing. The man demanded the doctors test him again. They said no, there was no reason, but the father insisted. So they shrugged and tested the son again, and of course, you can guess what happened. The cancer was gone.

The doctors continued to test him over and over again, but all his counts were normal, and it was as if he had never had leukemia in the first place. They

were so baffled that they wrote about the situation in
a medical journal.

When I finished the story, I looked down from the stage
at my daughters and asked if they had ever heard the story.
They hadn't. "I'm so sorry," I told them. I had no excuse.
That sick boy was their grandfather. My own dad. And
fifty-six years later, the cancer still has not come back.

I heard that story when I was a kid. I hadn't forgotten
about it over the years, but I hadn't exactly remembered
either. So I called up my parents in a last-second flash of
inspiration, and they gave me all the details.

Our attention spans are like that. They will gravitate
toward the sad, the broken, and all that is unfinished in the
world. That is why testimonies are so precious. The stories
of hope, big or small—from our neighbors or from our
own histories—are evidence of the hand of God. Without
them, we might despair.

But when we fix our eyes on those stories, forgetting
our current hardships if only for a moment, the opposite
happens: Joy. And joy is infectious. When we look for it in
others, we find it more at home.

This is how I beat back cynicism. I remind myself that
I am small, that the world is big, and that God has not
forgotten me.

Yes, my son has severe autism, and that can be immensely
difficult, but my life is shot through with blessing. Jack has
four siblings, for one thing, and they are all smart, adorable,

and kind. My daughters, Emily and Jenna, grow rich in compassion, and my sons, Sam and Nathan, are hell-bent on justice. These children are always active, always entertaining, and ever-forgiving of their bumbling dad.

There's my beautiful wife, too. Sara has been with me for eighteen years and hasn't left. She is probably the most selfless person I know.

What gifts I have. It's not fair!

And then there's Jack. Despite the paralyzing effects of his condition, he finds more delight in the simple things of this world than anyone I have ever met. The copper glimmer off a bean can, a simple tickle to the ribs. Give the boy a pair of socks, and he will be off jumping and giggling for hours on end.

It's not fair.

It's not fair that he is so kind to his brothers, or that he is so patient with us when we don't understand him, or that he never, ever holds a grudge against anyone for being irritated. He flashes that pure smile, that unfiltered delight, and we are all Play-Doh in his palms, because we adore this child, and in his own wordless way, he adores us too.

And none of it is fair. God's love toward us is so extravagant and undeserved. His mercies, new at every sunrise, float through our home like a morning mist. We breathe it in, even on the days we can't see it. In that joyful air, we live and move and have our being.

CHAPTER 12

Digging Up the Shallow Grave

JACK USED TO LOVE THE WATER more than anything else on the planet. On early summer days, he would don his favorite blue, skintight wet suit in hopes of earning a trip to the community pool. We always laughed, because he had outgrown the suit, and the tight fit was verging on scandalous. But we would take him, and he would jump and splash in the shallows for hours on end. A happier boy you'd have never seen.

Then, when he was eight years old and that big regression came, he forgot it all. He no longer wanted to swim anywhere, and he would recoil at the mere mention of the word *pool*. We could hardly get him in the bathtub. It was a sad thing to watch an old joy turn into something scary.

At last, on one early autumn afternoon at the local state park, he told us the problem. I had wanted to put him on my back and walk with him into the lake, but he tensed up and kicked his legs, shouting, "Great white shark! Great white shark!"

It was a eureka moment for the entire family. We all gasped and looked at one another with big, sad smiles. Jack had been watching the wrong kinds of cartoons.

"Oh, buddy! There are no sharks in the lake. *Wild Kratts* is just pretend. You don't have to be scared."

He listened and wanted to believe us. God help him, he was trying. We could see it all over his face. I scooped him up, and we tiptoed down into the ripples. His body was taut at first, but I could feel his limbs relax with every step. Within a half hour, he was splashing about like a river otter at feeding time.

I'll always remember that afternoon as the sudden climax of a haunting scenario: the transformation of a great joy into a great terror, then back again. I felt a familiar irony in that story. After all, I, too, had come to fear something I was yearning for.

For years, I had been avoiding a man named Rich. I knew him by reputation, having met him just once or twice in casual settings. By all accounts, he was a great guy—a college minister with a great sense of humor and a wonderful family. But still, I ducked him until our mutual friend, Jeff, forced the issue.

We were on a pastoral prayer retreat in the town of Cannon Beach, one of my favorite spots in all of Oregon. Every year, we begin our three-day venture with "the walk to

the rock," in which we pair up and take a long stroll down
the beach until we get to the spectacular Haystack Rock.
It's at least a mile away, so there is plenty of time to get
acquainted, open up a little bit, and pray for one another.

Jeff saw that I hadn't found a walking partner yet, so he
called out to me, "Hey, Jason, why don't you join us?" He
was standing next to Rich.

I tried not to groan. "Cool, thanks."

The sun was out, and the wind was light. It was a perfect afternoon, except for the pressing weight I felt in my
soul as I listened to Rich's story. His son, AJ, was autistic.
As a boy, AJ had been a lot like Jack. He had been nonverbal and altogether noncommunicative. But now, years
later, everything was different. AJ the autistic teenager did
not live in a fog like he used to. On the contrary, he was
happy and downright chatty with his family. He was intelligent and exuberant, interesting and funny.

I had heard a bit of this story already, which was why
I had ducked Rich for so long. It was too enticing a testimony. Too hopeful. If their journey had been darker, I
might have reacted differently, but the prospect of hearing
such a glowing report made my stomach groan. I didn't
need more false treasure maps in my life.

Now, though, I couldn't avoid him any longer. I
couldn't hide from the testimony of God breaking through
for someone very much like my son.

AJ's breakthrough hadn't come quickly, we learned. His
parents had researched until they discovered a methodology

that intrigued them. The concept was simple enough: Instead of trying to pull AJ out of his private world, they would let that world thrive, and they would try to enter into it.

"Think of it as 'incarnational parenting,'" Rich explained. That was language I could understand. Jesus didn't try to pull us into the heavenly realm so we could see all that we were missing. No, he incarnated—he put on flesh—and entered into our world. He found a door. Maybe we could find a door to reach Jack, too.

The concept of "entering into his world" wasn't new to us. We had heard it before, and we had tried our best to get through to our son by taking an interest in his favorite things. Rich and his wife, Monica, though, had successfully made a practice of it.

First, they had prepared a room of the house especially for AJ so he could escape the swirling noise and cluttered visages of normal family life. They encouraged him to spend regular time in that room away from his brothers. One parent would go with him. Then, for hours every day, they would do all the same things he did. They would not disturb his routines with words but would instead follow his lead. They would physically copy him.

AJ was six years old when they started. For weeks, nothing happened. They would take turns sitting next to him and watching him drop his action figures onto a mattress. They would drop action figures too.

Then, one afternoon, seven weeks into this new routine,

AJ stopped what he was doing and turned to look at Rich, who was in the middle of dropping an action figure, and asked, "Dad, what are you doing?" The words were intelligent, clean, and pure.

Rich froze. AJ had never spoken with such clarity. "I'm just playing," Rich said, making an effort to keep his voice level.

"Oh," his son replied, then turned back to his action figures.

The dominoes all fell after that. AJ started talking, playing with his brothers, reading books, and sharing his own delights with the world he used to hide from. It didn't happen overnight, but it happened. He was still autistic, of course. He will always be autistic, able to see the world from fascinating angles we neurotypicals can hardly fathom and grappling to interface with our strange, paradoxical culture. But he had already overcome the most severe symptoms that had once paralyzed him. The road would be long, but AJ had a future.

Sara and I took in the tale with antsy, aching hearts. It had only been two months since I preached on answered prayers, and the lesson had taken root. I wasn't resentful toward God, and I didn't begrudge other people for their successes either. So when I heard Rich's story, I was happy for my new friends. Really, I was.

But the story also did precisely what I feared it would do. It tempted me—no, dared me—to believe in an old truth I had tried hard to put to rest: that there might yet be more for my son than what I was waiting for.

Thus, the walk to the rock became my "great white shark" moment. I realized I had been hiding from the thing I wanted most. The more Rich talked, the more my heart kicked and thrashed inside me, pointing and screaming at the thing I had taught myself to fear: "Hope! Hope!"

Did I dare believe again that Jack might come out of his fog with the gifts of language and conversation? Did I dare imagine a future for him outside his living room sanctuary?

No, it was too much to entertain. I had traveled this path before, and I knew where it dead-ended. My soul remembered the exhausting war between acceptance and breakthrough. I didn't want to go back there to wade the old waters of disappointment. I didn't need hope anymore. I had found joy, and that was enough for me. I had found it in the distant promise of Restoration Day and in the close-up, small victories of everyday living. I found it in God's deep, churning, "I am with you" presence and in the embrace of those who loved me most. I had even learned to join in on other people's parties.

My soul had learned to exhale, in other words. I had found contentment. But it had come at the expense of my daydreams.

In my younger years, I was always thinking about future possibilities. Like many in the international missions community, I had fancied myself a visionary. Our heroes were men like Hudson Taylor, John Wesley, and Saint Patrick. I was always on the lookout for the next big ideas, new strategic ventures, and fresh ways to change the world. That tendency often irritated my friends and coworkers who wanted me to focus on what was happening right in front of us. All I wanted to do was think about tomorrow.

But all those years later, I realized I couldn't do it anymore. Someone had asked me what my vision for ministry was. That is a common question in my circles—so common, in fact, that it verges on being cliché. Yet I could not find an answer. I reached inside for it, but nothing was there—no visions for what I might someday accomplish, or even of the great things my children might do. I didn't think about the future anymore. Forget projectors that display our rosy expectations; I had no picture at all. The only thing I had was a stark, empty screen.

Maybe you're the same way. Most of us loved to look forward, once upon a time. Childish optimism, visions of what might become real, pulsed through our veins. That's why so many of us wanted to be inventors or astronauts. We lived on planets with shrink rays, aliens, and lollipop trees. Anything was possible! Sure, such dreams were enhanced by Hollywood producers peddling pixie dust and pushing songs about wishing on a star, but those men were only building on what already existed inside us. We came into this world with visions of princesses, dragons, and knights who went on quests.

Our dreams were so naive then. We were so innocent. But it was all bound to die.

I was reflecting on childhood innocence last year while watching my son Sam at his baseball game. Whenever

his team was up to bat, he would raise his voice and sing
for the batter: "Let's go, Ezra, let's go!" (*Clap-clap.*) In an
instant, the whole team would join in on it. The chant
lasted throughout the entire game. Even when a batter
struck out, it continued in a modified form: "Way to go,
Ezra, way to go," and so on.

Such sweetness, unmarred by competitive instincts and
adolescent resentments, made my heart throb. I wanted to
bottle it up for a later time, because it cannot last. Childish
innocence, just like childish dreaming, never lasts. Our kids
will taste disillusionment, no matter how hard we try to
protect them from it. Soon that entire baseball team will
awaken to the brokenness both around them and within
them. It is inevitable.

When that brokenness finally comes and our children's
innocence dies, our job description changes forever. We
embrace them in their failure. We tell them, "All is not
lost," and we point a new way forward to new life. Our
deepest, truest work as parents is not to provide safety but
to assist in redemption.

I wonder if the same might be true of our dreaming,
the death of which seems to be as inevitable as the death of
innocence itself. Maybe there is new life there, too. Because
we need it. You and I both grew up and found the world
to be a harsher place than we ever expected. No amount of
pixie dust can lift us over our grown-up gravities: We aren't
quick enough to play in the NBA, outer space is too big to
explore, and our sons were diagnosed with severe autism.

We got hurt as we got older, and we decided it wasn't worth it to dream anymore.

But what if redemption exists not just for our broken-ness but also for our buried dreams? If that's true, then the real work of faith begins *after* we bury them, not before. It is after disillusionment strikes that we need to learn what it means to have faith in something—to venture back into our half-wrecked worlds with fresh confidence, however tepid, that God might yet make beauty from ashes.

This was, I realized, my only way forward. I had buried my hopes in an imagined cemetery years earlier and called it all "rubble." I had laid to rest my dreams that Jack could ever kick out the walls of his prison and let his voice be heard.

Oh, what tragic agreements we make with ourselves! All those secret decisions, those wordless promises can reverberate inside us for years after we make them. I was blind to what I had done. But now, as we listened to AJ's story, it seemed that God was offering redemption.

Those couple of days were rough. I felt as broken as I had ever been, and my wife took the brunt of it. We don't argue often, but we did that week. We fought, we listened, then we fought some more, and finally, we prayed. And after we prayed, I knew the answer: I had to dig up the shallow grave. It was time to join my wife in trusting not only in God's care but also in Jack's ability to learn and grow. It was time to find the doors into Jack's world, enter through those doors, and believe.

When we came home from the prayer retreat, we cleared out a room upstairs and started taking him there for a couple of quiet hours every afternoon. He still loved to flap socks or lanyards more than anything else, but we knew that wasn't going to be enough, because we had tried that. He wasn't looking at his flappers; he was closing one eye and looking through them toward his favorite things. And all his favorite things were movie related.

This, we decided, was the key. His movies were the door to everything. Laminated pictures of his favorite movie covers lined every inch of our bookshelves for easy, continuous flapping. His words, when he spoke, were nearly always echoes of his favorite quotes. They were garbled, but the accents were unmistakable.

So we took armfuls of DVD cases upstairs, along with his stuffed animals, cars with eyes on them, and laminated screenshots featuring flying dragons. That was all it took to make the room feel comfortable.

Every day, we took turns with him. Some days it was pure quietness. He would arrange his disks in a way that made sense to him, and we would flap together in relative silence. Or we would take the whiteboard and work together on copying what we saw on one of his movie covers: a flying house and a cluster of balloons beside the word *Up*. On other days, he would lie down, and we would curl up next to him and take a nap.

We were hoping for a "Dad, what are you doing?" moment like the one AJ had, but of course, things never happen the same way twice. What happened was this: Jack became more comfortable with us than before, and this created new opportunities for communication.

"What do you want to talk about today, Jack?" we would ask him on his walk home from school. We knew the answer would be movie related, so we gave him a choice. "Do you want to talk about *Ratatouille* or *Kung Fu Panda*?"

He would perk up. "*Kung Fu Panda*."

It was an opening, and we would walk through it, launching into memories about Po and Tigress and Master Shifu. He would listen and smile, even if he didn't chime in. I think he could tell that we were taking more interest in his favorite things, and it showed. He was hearing us, and he was liking it.

So we dove in even more to Jack's borrowed mythology: *Toy Story* and *How to Train Your Dragon*, *The Incredibles* and *Despicable Me*. We were already familiar with all of these, but they were taking on new worth now, so we paid more attention.

His favorite film was, unfortunately, the one that drove the rest of us a little batty: Disney • Pixar's *Cars 2*. None of us liked the movie. We found it obnoxious and loud, not to mention incomprehensible.

One night, my daughters, Emily and Jenna, were sitting in the living room with him, attempting the same conversations we always tried.

"Jack, do you like *Cars 2* or *Despicable Me 2*?" Jenna asked.

He stopped flapping. "*Cars 2*," he said.

Jenna sighed. "Yeah, I like *Despicable Me 2* better. It's funnier."

"Yeah—sorry, Jack." Emily jumped in. "We don't really like *Cars 2* very much."

At that, he put his flappers down and spoke to them in a garbled, vaguely Russian accent: "Okay, just because everybody hates it doesn't mean it's not good!"

There was a pause, and then the room exploded with laughter. We all recognized the line and the accent. It was what Gru had said to his assistant, Dr. Nefario, after tasting his jelly recipe in *Despicable Me 2*. Jack had lifted the line and put it in perfect context in order to defend his favorite movie.

This wasn't the first time he had done this. Remember, he used to cry, "Daddy, help me!" when the bath water would drain from the tub—a reference to *Finding Nemo*. Now, though, the whole family was both pursuing him and paying more attention. I think he knew it, because the quotes kept coming.

"Jack," Emily said on another night, "it's time to brush your teeth and get your pajamas on."

He was visibly irritated, like all kids are at bedtime, and he responded with another Russian-ish Gru line: "You've got to be pulling on my leg!"

The quotes came in other contexts, too, like trips to the doctor. One afternoon, he was scheduled for an MRI. Sara tried to explain ahead of time how he was going to be inside a strange, tube-shaped machine, and he wasn't excited about it. But he would be asleep anyway. We knew that was our only option; there's no way this boy would willingly be still for so long.

He said nothing as the medical team prepared him— nothing they could understand, anyway. Then the moment came to administer the gas that would put him to sleep. He resisted at first but then gave in. When the medicine started to take effect, he looked at Sara and reshaped a husky line from Pumbaa, the warthog sidekick in *The Lion King*: "I told you this wasn't a good idea." And then he fell asleep. The doctors and nurses gasped and looked at Sara; it was the last thing they had ever expected.

"It's okay, you can laugh," she said, and they all did.

Another time, he had a sleep study at the hospital. He was lying on the edge of the bed with a tangled web of elec- trodes stuck to his head and chest. Sara curled up next to him to calm his squirming, and the nurse lifted the metal guard so he wouldn't fall off the mattress.

When Jack realized he couldn't get out, he spoke with the voice of Winnie the Pooh. Remember the scene when Pooh tries to escape Rabbit's house after eating too much? Jack did: "Oh, oh, help and bother! I'm stuck," he said.

There is no need to exaggerate the breakthrough. Sometimes his quotes still came out at random times, and it was clear he was just talking to himself. But other times, his intention was clear. He was communicating with us. He didn't have his own words, so he borrowed them from his animated friends. Movies were not just his favorite diversions anymore—they were becoming his emotional vocabulary.

Months passed. These sparks of communication started coming more frequently, and Sara pounced on the momentum. She started to take "upstairs time" to a new level by focusing less on flapping and more on coaxing new information from him. She would start with movies, of course, asking either/or questions about plots and characters from the stories he had memorized.

But of course, this was all surface-level stuff. She wanted to know what was going on inside of him. In this season, for instance, we knew he was having a hard time at school. His teachers were doing their best, but when he went to the mainstream class with kids his age, he would get stressed out and make all kinds of noise. One of his classmates got irritated with him and lashed out with the words "Jack is stupid!"

Jack screamed the moment he heard the words. He was listening. Always listening. He was in there, and he had things to say.

So one day, after beginning with the standard movie-related interrogation, Sara shifted her line of questioning. "Let's talk about you, Jack. What do you want people to know about you?"

He didn't answer at first, so she tried a different tack. She lifted a line from another of Jack's favorite movies, a forgettable sequel entitled *The Lion King 1½*.

"Hey, I've got an idea," she said in the voice of Timon the

meerkat. "Why don't we tell 'em our story?" He looked up at her and seemed to understand. This was his native tongue.

Jack had been learning to read and write at a first grade level, though he was old enough to be in fourth, so Sara pulled out the whiteboard. *Jack is,* she wrote, and then stopped to give him options. He loved options. "Jack is what? Funny? Silly? What do you want us to know about you?"

He reached for the marker and took the whiteboard.

He wrote *S-M-A-R-T.*

It was a sobering message to all of us, but he had found a way to express it, and that brought a flood of excitement that pushed through even our sadness for him. It was aching joy in a single, written word. My son was finding his voice.

More words came after that. Through a blend of offered choices, verbal requests, an alphabet stencil, and our trusty whiteboard, Jack told us much about himself in the ensuing months. He told us that he liked to sing, that he wanted a cat, and that he loved it when we had family time, especially when we reenacted Winnie the Pooh's climactic escape from Rabbit's hole. The whole family would grab hands, sing the "Heave! Ho!" song, and pull him off the couch. Then I would fly him across the room and into the clothes dryer, our makeshift honey tree.

This was my son's world. It was not a blank, unthinking place after all. Rather, it was full of color and laughter and feeling, and he was letting us in.

For a while, I lamented the fact that he wasn't responding to me the way he was with Sara. He didn't want to do "work time" with me at all. I had very little success there. The minute I would come in and close the door, he would look at me and start laughing.

Then I realized what any other dolt would have seen right away: that this was a pretty cool arrangement for a dad. He didn't want to work with me; he wanted to play with me. So I started to oblige him more often.

"Sonnn," I would say in my best impression of the famed Viking Stoick the Vast from *How to Train Your Dragon*. "You've got to watch out for dragons!"

Jack's eyes would light up. The scene was always made up, but always familiar. A boy and his father.

"I don't know, Dad," I would say, switching to Hiccup's ever-quivering voice. "Dragons are . . . well . . . they're kind creatures, Dad!"

"Noooo, son!" I would yell in response, two inches from Jack's nose. He would be red-faced and laughing by then. "They are dangerous! See, here comes one right now!"

Then I would spin around and pull him onto my back, and we'd become Hiccup and Toothless, the dragon rider on his Night Fury. And together, we'd soar over carpets and hardwood; over stale disappointments and old, forgotten graves. We would fly as father and son over foggy histories, jagged sorrows, and the frozen wastelands of low expectations.

And I know the risks. We might still fall back into those landscapes. There is no pixie dust to keep either of us airborne. These are real dreams in the real world, and autism is a real disorder. Jack will move forward, but he will also move backward sometimes. He will fly high, but he will also crash.

I've decided, however, that these soaring moments are worth every bruise I may incur at the hands of disappointment. I cannot fear that feral beast any longer. I've seen too much now. Too much beauty. Too many surprises.

You shouldn't fear disappointment either. Hope needs to breathe. Dreams need redemption. And we serve a God who revitalizes both.

My old dreams died, but I have new ones now. I don't dream for a full restart anymore. No, my son is who he is, and I adore who he is. So now I dream that we will know more of him. All of him. I dream that he will keep kicking out the sides of his box until there is nothing left in his way. And I dream that people will come in—that he will make friends who understand him and see all the treasures God has laid in his soul.

This is my vision of hope restored. And I am watching it come to life.

Jack is still clinging to my back, and we fly around the table and back toward the living room. I yell again in Hiccup's voice, "This is amazing!"—because it really is amazing: a boy finding his voice, a family learning to listen, and the God of heaven helping a chronic doubter face eastward toward a new and inevitable dawn.

Epilogue

The Way of Aching Joy

IT'S A FORTY-ONE-MINUTE DRIVE to Jack's new school. He sits squinting at the sky in the back seat of our 2005-model Prius. His window comes down a crack, but it's starting to sprinkle, so I slide it up again, and he shrieks in protest.

"Okay," I concede. "But it's raining, so only open it a little."

He listens and complies. Something is making him laugh this morning. I don't know what it is. A funny shape in the clouds, maybe? Or is the air tickling his nose?

We push through the morning rush hour and begin to curl through the Oregon hills, crossing crystal rivers and bending green pastures. The distant forest fires have been smothering our whole region with a pillow of smoke, but today the air is clean and clear—a welcome blessing, a good gift from above.

It all feels so familiar. And it all feels so different. Jack is not the same boy he was in the early days. Even though words still don't come easily to him, he has opened his world to us now. Bit by bit, he is letting us in.

But autism is unpredictable. It's been two weeks, and Jack still hasn't so much as stepped inside the classroom of his new school. He isn't throwing fits and he isn't melting down. He just . . . won't go in. He stands out in the hallway and watches as the other kids—all of them on the spectrum themselves—work and play and interact with their specialist teachers. It's a beautiful environment, but the change has so far been too much for him, and we are all a little on edge. While I drive, I pray that today will be the day.

The line of yellow buses signals our arrival, and we slip past them to the second entrance.

"Orange home?" he says when we stop. That is what he has called our house ever since we moved from a green one five years ago.

"Nope. School time," I say, getting out and opening his door.

"Nofankyou!" he yells.

"First school, then orange home," I insist, and he gets out, because he knows it's a lost cause.

We find his earphones and sunglasses. He puts them on, and I hand him the chart that Sara printed earlier this morning. Twenty minutes in the classroom will earn him one movie after school. That's a good trade, I remind him. Just twenty minutes. Come on, son!

But I can see it on his face. He has no interest in trades today.

We walk together down the long hallway, and he opens his locker without prompting, slipping his backpack inside.

His teacher emerges from the room. "Good morning, Jack," she says and immediately tries to send him on a simple, harmless errand into the classroom.

"Nofankyou!"

I look at her and shrug. She's been so patient. They all have. They're trying everything, but the boy has a will of iron. Yesterday he sat for hours in the doorway itself, unwilling to slide the extra few inches into a new season of life and joy. Even the other kids tried to coax him in, assuring him that everybody gets scared sometimes and that everything would be okay, but he would not be moved. Bravery takes effort. He didn't want to be brave just then. He only wanted to escape.

I think of that image of my son on the floor, and I see myself. How many times have I chosen to sit in a hallway instead of entering the mystery?

When facing challenges, we can pray prayers of deliverance or prayers of endurance. Most of us, at least here in the West, lean heavily on the former. We want out of the situation, so we ask God to make it all better, to calm the storm, to make the pain go away.

There's nothing wrong with praying prayers of deliverance. However, the New Testament writers prayed prayers of endurance at least as often. The apostles repeatedly prayed for boldness in the face of persecution and patience in the face of suffering. Did they ask God to deliver them from difficult situations? Certainly. But they also asked for the wisdom and wherewithal to navigate those situations: "Lord, give me strength to go through this new doorway."

Maybe it's because I grew up not knowing crises, but when hardships come, my first inclination is still to say, "Lord, fix this" instead of "Lord, help me." It's all well and good to pray, "God, take the pain away," but what about "God, help me endure the pain"? I don't pray that way very often. I just want the tension to go away.

It hasn't yet. Even after all his breakthroughs—after "Jack and Daddy" and all the movie lines and whiteboard moments—the tension continues to do its worst. I want so badly for it to stop. I want my questions answered. I want God to be there standing by, ready to solve our mysteries like a cosmic Sherlock Holmes, ready to airlift us out of our crises like a first responder: my own personal search-and-rescue God.

But alas, he's not here to do my bidding, and even if he were, there would still be something amiss in those desires. They don't fit reality. It doesn't matter how we feel—the Scriptures assure us that the tension will remain. The same Jesus who said signs and wonders will follow us also assured us that in this world we will have trouble (see Mark 16:17; John 16:33). Likewise, the same apostle Paul who urged us to have patience in suffering also told us to exercise the victorious gifts of the Holy Spirit (see Romans 5:3-4; 1 Corinthians 12:4-11).

Our world, then, will never be one-dimensional. Here, victory and defeat comingle. Here, weddings and funerals occur under the same roof. The world is full of both beauty and brokenness, of question marks and exclamation points, of smooth roads and potholes. Tension and mystery are sewn into the tapestry of creation, and they will last to the end of the age.

I used to think that if God ironed out the one great wrinkle in my life, I could jettison all my anxieties forever. I thought if he would "come through" for my son, then I could go on being happy and carefree all my days.

In my heart, though, I knew it couldn't be true. Even if God granted a sudden miracle and Jack had a complete breakthrough—even if every barrier between my son and the world crumbled in a heartbeat—I would still find brokenness around me. There would be another crisis to weigh me down—a new sickness, a sudden loss, a relational breakdown—and I would be shaken again.

What a strange realm we find ourselves in. One gift received, another withheld. The Land of Unanswered Prayer is a paradoxical place: Some prayers actually do get answered, despite what we've named this place, and some do not. The future is unpredictable, and that can be disconcerting. We don't know what might lie around the next bend.

However, that same truth presents a wild invitation

to adventure and surprise. We don't know what might lie around the next bend! We don't know what wayside treasures God has prepared for us. We can't see the streams of refreshing, the encouragement of the saints, or the victories that await us at the bridges of hope redeemed. Even in the nighttime hours, he offers us all these treasures of the dark.

We will never fully escape the Land of Unanswered Prayer until Restoration Day. So for now, we walk this country with eyes and hearts wide open. Rather than trying to dodge all the inevitable pain, we enter into it. We choose to feel it all. And because we make that choice, we feel all the good that comes with it, too.

The way of aching joy isn't a sentimental way of experiencing life; it is the very way of Christ. We follow him, the Man of Sorrows, who for the joy set before him endured the aching of the cross. He knew what waited for him on the hill of the skull, yet he set his face like flint and marched straight toward it. He did it for joy. For the joy of being with us forever.

A mystery? Yes. It is the ultimate mystery. The Prince of Heaven—the favored Son of the Celestial Citadel—traded his glory to enter into our temporal pains. Why he did it still confounds me. I am hardly a breath, and my pains, heavy though they seem, are a blip.

Nevertheless, he came and met me, and you, and he still meets us on the cold sands of this in-between country. We sit in a doorway, and he calls us forward to rise up and walk toward the paradox, to enter into the mystery of all that is unfinished.

And sometimes, against all odds, we find that he has indeed answered us. We see that he heard our deep longings all along. Sara and I, more than anything else, just wanted to know our son. We cried out to God for that gift. We felt like he was yanked away from us, and we wanted to share in his life.

Today, we are sharing in his life, and he is sharing in ours.

One summer weekend, I grabbed some friends and dragged them, along with Jack, to a forgotten beach on Oregon's central coast. There, under a perfect sky and a crystal yellow sun, we filmed a video. My friend Robert put his drone in the air, and it soared over Jack while he stared out at the water. I watched Jack from behind, and while the cameras rolled, I recited a poem I'd written.[1]

"What do the waves mean, son of mine?"

I asked the question repeatedly, turning it over to reflect different shades of meaning and frustration. There are the waves of outrage in the autism community over what labels we use, or who gets to talk and when. There are the waves of progress and regress that knock down dreams like sandcastles. There are the ever-growing swells of medical riddles: anxiety on top of OCD on top of epilepsy on top of autism.

So many questions. I want to understand them all.

But for all my reoccurring frustrations, I am certain that Jack has far more. We only have to find the door into one world. For him, every door is strange. Every interaction is tiring and probably seems foreign. He has to fight hard for every little gain, and then he has to clutch onto it before it gets lost in the next regression.

Jack's life is full of far more tension than mine, and yet you should see how he faces his waves. You should watch him flapping at the sea. His wrists swirl, and his face is full of exhilaration and delight. It is as if he's reciting poems with his palms, telling fables with his fingertips. This boy is full of more gladness than anyone I know.

"Can you teach me how to wade these waters with winsome eyes and a laughing chin?" I asked in the poem. Because that's what he does on most days. He stands in the way of tension and jumps up and down on his toes.

I want to be like him. I want to giggle in the winds of lingering uncertainty. I want to be brave.

It took a while for Jack to remember that winsome posture at his new school, but he did, eventually. His teachers put a line of tape just inside the classroom door, and for hours, he sat there with his feet stretched out to that line. And little by little, they pulled the tape further into the classroom.

It took a lot of patience and a lot of prayer, but he did it. He made it through the doorway, past the weeks of tension, and into his unknown. And when he did it, his classmates and teachers cheered him on, for he had scored a great victory.

He returned to orange home like a conquering hero of

aching joy, worthy of a double portion both of piggyback rides and of movies. And he knew he had done something special too. It was all over his smile.

The apostle Paul encapsulated how to walk the way of aching joy: "Rejoice in hope," he said, "be patient in tribulation, be constant in prayer" (Romans 12:12, ESV).

We rejoice, because there is indeed hope.

We are patient, because there is indeed tribulation.

And we stay constant in prayer, because there is indeed a God who listens. There is a Father who trains us to embrace the tension and make a friend of mystery. There is a Savior who meets us at our places of pain and teaches us to laugh the laugh of the redeemed.

The video we shot exploded on the weekend I uploaded it. It took only four days to garner over a million views. I wasn't prepared for the outpouring of affection I received from other parents of special-needs children all over the world. I didn't write the poem for them, after all. I wrote it for Jack. I wrote it to express my affection for him.

Still, they expressed over and over again how they heard their own voices in it, especially in the closing lines:

"You are not a disorder, my son," I said, still watching as my boy played tag with the waves that rolled up to his toes.

"But neither are you normal. No. You're a piece of God's own daydreams, a reflection of aching joy.

"No, you're not normal.

"You are . . . beloved."

And at that, I gave up talking and ran after my beloved

boy, tossed him in the air, and cradled him in my arms. Then we ran into the waves together and danced.

When parents saw it, they said they felt their own swirling mixtures of sadness and hope. Their situations are not easy, but when they see the smiles of their precious children, they remember the deep, abiding, unconditional affection inside them. In those smiles, they find new gladness to face new days.

On a deeper level, though, I think they felt something that I neither alluded to nor ever intended: I think they heard a whisper from their own Father as they watched. Even many who don't remember him, or don't believe in him at all, can sometimes still feel that familiar pull inside them. We all lean toward our True North. We were created for the warmth of our Father's arms. It is the only place where we find shelter against the cold winds of emotional chaos and conflicting truths.

If there is an answer to the mysteries and tensions in this unfinished life, we will not find it in philosophy or poetry or self-help religion. Rather, we only find it in a Person.

When Jack is aching, he can't always find his words, but he always knows who to come to. He finds his mother or his father. He takes our hands and brings us to his place of pain. Then he leans into us and lets go under the weight of our hands, even if the pain lingers.

And the Savior said, "You must become like little children" (Matthew 18:3, author's paraphrase).

What does that mean for you, friend? Your pains could

vanish, or they could linger. The healing you've been praying for or the loss you've been dreading . . . either one
might become real in an instant. Or there might be no
resolution at all. You might wait under these same circumstance for weeks or months or years.

Nevertheless, "rejoice in hope, be patient in tribulation,
be constant in prayer." Aching joy would be impossible
if we were self-sustaining adults, but fortunately, we are
much smaller than that. We are children of an eternal King.
Courage and healing are in his hands, and he waits for you
to call. He waits for you to tell him where it is you ache
and to rest under the shelter of his touch.

Some days, we forget it all, and we sit in the doorway
before the endless chaos of the churning sea, biting our
nails in fear of the future and in frustration over our own
continued weaknesses.

But not today. Today, we see our Father, and we run
to him. He touches our brokenness, tosses us high over
the mysteries, and wraps us up in his infinite warmth.
Together, we leap into the waves, stomping and splashing
and spinning round and round through the frigid Pacific.
The wind is cold but it will not overtake us. The waters are
hungry but they will not swallow us up. Not today. Not
with him.

No. Today, our Father's ancient feet dance beneath us
both, and his chest rumbles with a deep laughter forged
before the foundation of the world and all its seas. And
while we hear it, we laugh until we cry.

A Note to the Autism Community

I REALIZE HOW IMPORTANT language is to our community. In these pages, I have opted to use the term *autistic* instead of *with autism* most of the time, since that seems to be the preferred term among most self-advocates I have encountered.

In general, I have endeavored to share my journey as it actually happened, not how I wish it had happened. I wish I had possessed a better attitude toward Jack's autism early on. Unfortunately, my story was a messy one, and I opted to include the messiness in this book. I realize that by doing that, I run a risk of offending some in our community with certain terminology, as in my early desire for "healing." However, I decided the benefits of honesty outweighed the risks. If I can help other parents—especially dads—identify what they are feeling instead of telling them the way they ought to feel, they might, in the end, be better equipped to love their children the way they ought to. They might, in other words, become better fathers.

Rest assured, my thoughts and feelings about the autism spectrum have morphed considerably over the years and will continue to morph, I'm sure. In the meantime, if I have stepped on any toes in these pages, I beg your patience, and I hope you will allow me some latitude.

Acknowledgments

THIS BOOK IS ABOUT A JOURNEY, but it is itself the product of a long journey that I never could have completed without the hopeful encouragement of the saints at Christ's Center Church. Thank you guys for sharing your lives and your prayers so lavishly.

Deep thanks to those friends who have held our hands and strengthened our backs as we walked through the Land of Unanswered Prayer: the Wagners, Nunns, Waldrops, Starrs, Davises, Oakeses, Millses, Kaisers, Whittakers, Vergaras, and of course, all our family in Texas and Minnesota. We love you all.

Since this is Jack's story and not just my own, I also want to thank those who have walked this path with him: Lori Hood, Teresa Donovan, Ashonalee Olinger, Beth Donovan, and all of his teachers and therapists, including Miss Florien, Miss Natalie, Miss Molly, Miss Kendra, and his beloved Mrs. E. Thank you all.

To Rich, Monika, and AJ: Thank you for showing us what hope looks like and for letting us tell a bit of your story.

George Nita and Janae McWilliams: It was an honor to walk with you through the darkest hours. Thank you for letting me reflect on those experiences in these pages and for remaining part of our family. I love you both.

Thanks to Robert and Wendy Bearden, whose help in creating the video "A Reflection of Aching Joy" led in many ways to the creation of this book.

To Teresa Evenson, my agent: Thank you for taking a chance on me and for helping me understand what my story was really about all along.

To Caitlyn Carlson, my editor: Your enthusiasm for this book has meant as much to me as the skills you employed to make it better. Thank you for both gifts.

To Don Pape, Elizabeth Symm, the NavPress team, and everyone at Tyndale: I am so thankful for this collaboration, and I am honored to stand among you all. Truly.

To the Christ's Center pastoral staff: I shudder to think where I would be without you all. Doug Easterday, Red Crabb, and Jeff Starr, thank you for always reminding me how my Father sees me. Janell Wallis, thank you for prayerfully watching my back throughout this project and for dutifully kicking me out of my office twice a week to go write at Max Porter's. And Joshua and Karen Rivas, your insights into both the structure and content of this book were invaluable, and your caring friendship has refreshed and revived my heart more times over the years than I can possibly count. Thank you, guys. For everything.

Sam and Nathan: I know this was a long process, and it made Daddy crabby, but you still hugged me tight at the end of every day. Thank you for those hugs. I love you guys more than Cowboy Pete loves sheriffing.

Emily and Jenna: I'm sorry it took me so long to learn the truths I've put down in this book, and I'm sorry that I still forget them sometimes. Thank you for the patience you give me on my broody days, and for the compassion you give your brother every day. I'm proud of you both.

To Sara, whose love is fierce, whose wisdom is sharp, and

whose patience is a deep, deep well: Thank you for being my toughest critic and truest fan. You push me to be a better writer, a better father, and a better man. I adore you.

And finally, to Jack: I can only hope and pray this book will be a blessing to you, Son. Thank you for letting me write about us. And thank you for keeping your smile. I love you, my boy.

Soli Deo gloria.

Notes

CHAPTER 1: OUR PRECIOUS PROPAGANDA

1. This account of John was given by the early church father Tertullian: "The Apostle John was first plunged, unhurt, into boiling oil, and thence remitted to his island-exile!"; Tertullian, *Prescription against Heretics* (Pickerington, OH: Beloved, 2014), 47. For more on the fate of John and the other disciples, see Bryan Litfin, *After Acts: Exploring the Lives and Legends of the Apostles* (Chicago: Moody, 2015).

CHAPTER 2: A GATHERING STORM

1. Brian and Jenn Johnson, "You Have Ravished My Heart," *We Believe,* copyright © 2006 Bethel Music; see also Song of Solomon 4:9.
2. "Lorica of Saint Patrick," EWTN, accessed May 11, 2018, https://www .ewtn.com/Devotionals/prayers/patrick.htm.

CHAPTER 3: PSALMS OF LAMENT

1. See Genesis 18:16-33, Exodus 32:7-14, and Genesis 32:22-32, respectively.
2. See Isaiah 45:3.

CHAPTER 4: THE FORGETTING PLACE

1. R.E.M., "Everybody Hurts," *Everybody Hurts,* copyright © 1993 Warner Bros.

2. Laura Sanders, "Smartphones May Be Changing the Way We Think," *ScienceNews*, March 17, 2017, https://www.sciencenews.org/article /smartphones-may-be-changing-way-we-think.

3. See Revelation 12:10-11.

CHAPTER 5: PLANTING A GARDEN

1. "Mayo Clinic Minute: What Is Autism?," Mayo Clinic, April 13, 2017, https://newsnetwork.mayoclinic.org/discussion/mayo-clinic-minute -what-is-autism/.

2. *The Shawshank Redemption*, featuring Morgan Freeman and Tim Robbins (1994; Burbank, CA: Warner Home Video, 1999), DVD.

3. According to ESV.org, the reverse trip was "nearly 900 miles." ESV.org, accessed June 4, 2018, https://www.esv.org/resources/esv-global-study-bible /facts-ezra-7/.

4. See Jeremiah 28:1-4, 10-11 and Ezekiel 13.

CHAPTER 6: IT'S NOT ALL RUBBLE

1. See Isaiah 53:3, John 11:17-45, Luke 19:41-44, and Hebrews 5:7.

CHAPTER 7: THE IN-BETWEEN COUNTRY

1. "Autistic Girl Expresses Unimaginable Intelligence," *20/20*, video clip posted May 25, 2011, by Ichiban MacBean, 9:52, https://www.youtube .com/watch?v=vNZVV4Ciccg.

2. C. S. Lewis, *Mere Christianity: A Revised and Amplified Edition, with a New Introduction, of the Three Books* Broadcast Talks, Christian Behaviour, *and* Beyond Personality (San Francisco: HarperOne, 2009), 136–37.

3. Gilbert K. Chesterton, *Orthodoxy* (New York: John Lane Company, 1908), 298.

CHAPTER 8: THE PENGUIN INCIDENT

1. To access this blurb, visit http://www.jasonhague.com/2012/07/13 /why-no-my-son-is-not-rain-man/.

2. See Exodus 14:1-31, 1 Kings 18:16-46, Isaiah 38:1-8, and John 11:38-44, respectively.

3. C. S. Lewis, "The Gods Return to Earth," review of *The Fellowship of the Ring*, by J. R. R. Tolkien, accessed March 1, 2018, http://www.theonering .com/news/books/the-gods-return-to-earth-c-s-lewis-apos-review-of-the -fellowship-of-the-ring. Originally published in *Time and Tide* (August 14, 1954), 1082.

CHAPTER 9: "I AM WITH YOU"

1. Dr. Gregory A. Boyd and Edward K. Boyd, *Letters from a Skeptic: A Son Wrestles with His Father's Questions about Christianity* (Colorado Springs: David C Cook, 2008), 76–77.

CHAPTER 10: TO GIVE HIM A SUPERPOWER

1. *Ratatouille*, directed by Brad Bird and Jan Pinkava (Emeryville, CA: Pixar, 2007), DVD.
2. Thomas Chisholm, "Great Is Thy Faithfulness," 1923.

EPILOGUE: THE WAY OF ACHING JOY

1. To watch this video, visit https://www.facebook.com/jasonhaguewriter /videos/1072882106082738/.